VILLAGE AND COUNTRY RESIDENCES

AND HOW TO BUILD THEM

S. B. Reed

FOREWORD BY NATHANIEL TRIPP

THE LYONS PRESS

Originally published in 1878 by Orange Judd Company

First Lyons Press edition, June 2000

Printed in Canada

10 9 8 7 6 5 4 3 2 1

Library of Congress Cataloging-in-Publication
Data is available on file.

FOREWORD

In the year 1878, when Mr. S. B. Reed's popular book was first published, our nation was in the midst of an enormous transformation. The wounds of the Civil War were finally healing. During the nine years that had followed the driving of the golden spike at Promontory Point, tendrils of the iron road had felt their way to nearly every corner of the continent. We had become a mobile society, no longer linked to the ancestral land. We moved with the industry. We moved with the jobs. We needed new homes.

Among the many inventions of those times was the magazine, and it was here that Mr. Reed's designs first appeared. The magazine, the perfect forum for the burgeoning middle class of literate Americans, was also perfect for popularizing the notion that even a man of modest means could obtain housing for himself and his family, and not just any housing, but a finely finished home that reflected the pride and promise of the early Victorian era. This was a revolutionary idea. For as little as two hundred and fifty dollars, a three-room cottage would comfortably and tastefully enclose the young family, with the assumption that the means to add on would be obtained later. Eight thousand dollars would build a mansion worthy of the most distinguished gentleman in town, a home as ornate as the bodice and bustle of the ladies of the day.

While some Americans would promenade, others would be hard at work. Another invention of the time was the circular "buzz" saw, powered by a steam engine. Lumber production was no longer the slow work of waterwheels and up-and-down saw. Timber harvesting had become industrialized. Now great swaths were being cut through the vast virgin pine stands of Michigan, sawn into timbers and boards of uniform dimension, and loaded onto railroad cars headed east, west, south, and across the treeless Great Plains.

Reed's designs themselves reflect the changing society. Gone are the small, boxlike apartments of colonial days. Instead, there is a new open feeling, more free of form, with hallways, lobbies, and wide doorways. Even the smallest home could be a man's castle. Reed went so far with this theme that he even recommended that bell cords and speaking tubes should be installed in the homes of mechanics and laborers on mere twenty-five-foot-wide lots. One of his loveliest of designs included here is for a block of row houses for the enlightened landlord. No matter how modest the home, there was always room for a decorative flourish or two at the peak, the eaves, or the entranceway.

Construction styles were in transition, too, and it may be that here Mr. Reed falters. He is, after all, an architect, not a builder, and quite an opinionated one at that. He refuses to accept the balloon framing style that was revolutionizing home building at the time, replacing post and beam, and making house framing a simple and standardized procedure. Instead he insists upon his own hybrid version, using an unpredictable mix of timber dimensions.

Today, such quirkiness on his part only adds to the book's charm. Hear him on the subject of squeaky stairs: "Squeaky stairs are abominable, and even when assured of their safety, one feels an instinctive suspicion of danger and will look for treachery in every part of the house." He also claimed to have invented machine-planed "novelty" siding, a radiator for wood stoves, and fool-proof rain gutters. These were considered great innovations in those days, before power tools, before sheetrock and plywood, before the word "suburbia" existed. He includes formulas for making your own paint, and the proper proportions of both animal hair and beef suet in your plaster. But best of all are his drawings.

In this great expansive age, when transatlantic travel was no longer such a dreaded ordeal, European styles were popular. Reed's wonderful designs, which epitomize the Victorian era, tend to favor the Italianate. What had been just a front porch was now a piazza. But there are also some fine examples of Second Empire and glimpses of Carpenter Gothic and stick built as well. It is on the inside, however, that the modern man will find certain facilities lacking. It is not until one gets to the most expensive homes that a bathroom is to be found, and central heating and insulation are still in the future as well. Nonetheless, piazza in front, privy out back, there is a house here for everybody.

—Nathaniel Tripp
St. Johnsbury, Vermont, 2000

PREFACE.

The flattering commendations received from nearly every part of the United States, and Canada, in reference to the House-plans published in the *American Agricul- turist* during the past three years, show that they meet a great want, and in response to a general demand, they are here presented in a convenient, connected form. The opportunity has been improved to make revisions, especially in most of the estimates, which were found necessary, owing to depreciation in the cost of building since their first issue. The author has been guided in this work by many years' experience, in planning and superintending the erection of country buildings, and has selected, from an extensive aggregation of original designs in his possession, such examples as seemed best to serve for purposes of simplicity, comfort, and economy. All the matters here presented are purely practical—well calculated to assist such as are contemplating the erection of either a village or country house. The plans embrace almost every variety of arrangement and style—each one is accompanied with a detailed description of its conveniences and construction—and its cost is shown by careful estimates, made to correspond with a uniform standard of prices, at present rates. To builders, this work will be valuable as a hand-book of reference, to aid them when applied to for suggestions, either in the projection of new dwellings, or in the alteration of old ones, saving much time, study, and calculations.   S. B. REED.

Corona, L. I., 1878.

CONTENTS.

DESIGN I.

Fig. 1.—EXTERIOR OF COTTAGE.

A COTTAGE, COSTING $250.

This plan was designed for a simple cottage, with sufficient accommodations for beginners in housekeeping with limited means. It is arranged as the *Wing* of a larger house to be erected in the future, as indicated in the dotted sketch adjoining the ground-plan. (The building, with the proposed enlargements complete, are given

in Design VIII. To a certain extent, one's dwelling is
an index of his character. Any effort at building expresses the owner's ability, taste, and purpose. Every
industrious man, starting in life, has a right, and should
be encouraged, to anticipate prosperity, as the sure re-
ward of honest worth ; and he may, with propriety, give
emphasis to such anticipations in every step, and with
every blow struck. His dwelling may well express the
progressive character, rather than a conclusive result.
Beginning a home by starting with a room or two, as
present means will allow, and increasing its dimensions
as can be afforded, without the precarious aid of the
money-lender, is honest, independent, and best provides
against the ever-changing vicissitudes of life. The first
step towards building is the preparation of plans. These
should be sufficiently comprehensive to embrace all
probable requirements. If only a small beginning is
intended, it should be made to exhibit some degree of
completeness, and be arranged to conform with the proposed future enlargements without serious alterations . . . .
EXTERIOR, (fig. 1). —In view of the relation this structure is to bear to a proposed main house, and to allow
for the grading likely to be required in the ultimate
completion of the whole, the foundation is made to show
four feet above the ground. Such elevation adds to the
prominence and good appearance of the building, and
relieves the interior from the dampness likely to result
from a closer contact with the soil. The style is simple,
neat, and favorable for the using of ordinary materials
and methods of construction . . . . INTERIOR, (fig. 2). —
Hight of ceiling, 9 feet. The entire floor space is util-
ized in the three convenient divisions—a Living-room,
Bedroom, and a Large Pantry—with no chimney-breast,
or stairway to interfere. Each room is pleasantly lighted,
and the larger one has outside entrances front and rear.
With a favorable location, the living-room may be made

a very cheerful apartment.... CONSTRUCTION. — For economy, and in prospect of a future enlargement, that shall include ample cellars, such excavations are omitted for this building. The Foundations are brick piers, extending in the earth below the reach of frost, and 4 feet above, and the intermediate spaces are close-boarded, making an inclosure useful for many purposes. If desired,

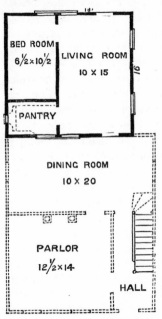

a sort of temporary cellar may be made, by deepening the central portion of this inclosure a foot or two, and banking the loose earth against the inside of the boarding. The Framework and other parts are substantially constructed, of materials as indicated in the appended estimate. The Chimney rests on the central partition (which is strengthened by the central pier of the foundation), and has two flues, with metal thimbles in the bottom of each—one to receive the stove-pipe from the living-room, and the other to serve as a ventilator for the bedroom. All

Fig. 2.—INTERIOR OF COTTAGE.

of the materials are intended to be of merchantable quality. The siding, flooring, and casings are mill-dressed. The sizes of the sash are 2 ft. 8 in. × 5 ft. 2 in., and of the doors, 2 ft. 8 in. × 6 ft. 8 in., all 1¹/₄ in. thick, and may be found ready-made, and seasoned, in the stock of any regular dealer.... In the following *estimate*, the item of $20, for carpenter's labor, may seem very little. This amount is allowed for preparing the building ready for the plasterer, and is entered in this manner for convenience in making the calculations. Adding to the above amount the cost of such labor in the " completed" parts, will make a total of $50.

Estimate, cost of materials and labor:

1,000 bricks, laid, at $12 per M	$12.00
124 yards plastering, at 20c. per yard	24.80
636 feet of timber, at $15 per M	9.54

2 sills, 4×6 in. 18 ft. long.	1 girder, 4×6 in. 18 ft. long.
2 sills, 4×6 in. 16 ft. long.	9 beams, 3×6 in. 16 ft. long.
4 posts, 4×6 in. 10 ft. long.	14 ceiling boards, 2×4 in. 16 ft. long.

75 wall-strips, 2×4×13, at 11c. each	8.25
98 siding, 9¼ inches, at 25c. each	24.50
Cornice materials	6.00
50 shingling lath, at 5c. each	2.50
6 shingling planks, at 20c. each	1.20
12 bunches shingles, at $1.25 per bunch	15.00
36 flooring, 9¼ in., at 25c	9.00
7 windows, complete, at $6	42.00
4 doors, complete, at $5	20.00
2 stoops and closets, complete	20.00
Nails, $4; painting, $14; carting, $5	23.00
Carpenter's labor, not included above	20.00
Incidentals	12.21
Total cost	$250.00

DESIGN II.

COUNTRY COTTAGE, COSTING $450 TO $550.

This plan of an inexpensive country dwelling is adapted to the wants of many people whose circumstances will not admit of a larger outlay. It was originally prepared and published in response to many calls for very low-priced country houses, "some as cheap as lumber and nails can make them." The present one approximates that point, and will aid in devising others.... Two Elevations are given for the same ground-plan; the first (fig. 3) is for a one-story house of the simplest design, with an entrance door, a neat porch, and two windows in front. The rear is arranged similarly. The roof is conspicuous, in keeping with its importance. No matter how cheaply one proposes to build a house, it is essential not to slight the roof. A roof fit for a one-story cottage would answer equally well on a three-story house,

Fig. 3.—ELEVATION OF ONE-STORY HOUSE.

so that relatively the cost of this part becomes greater, as the other parts become reduced and cheapened . . . . Ground-Plan, (fig. 4).—The accommodations are quite sufficient for a small family, consisting of three rooms, two lobbies, a kitchen-pantry, and a clothes-press. The Lobbies protect the rooms from direct contact with the outside doors. The Living-room is large, and accessible alike from each entrance ; it has windows front and rear, and is convenient to the pantry ; one entire side is unbroken, giving additional space for furniture, etc. The Pantry is shelved on two sides, and has a sash opening from the rear lobby, receiving light through the head-

light over the rear entrance door. The front Bedroom
is of good size—large enough to be used as a sitting-
room ; it adjoins the rear bedroom, and a clothes-press,
and has a window facing the road. The rear Bedroom is
the most retired, and has a window looking to the rear.
The Press or closet is shelved and hooked in the usual
manner. The door between the bedrooms might be dis-
pensed with, but its convenience more than repays its
cost.... CONSTRUCTION.—The Foundations are of common stone and
mortar, laid in
trenches, so as
not to be affect-
ed by frost, and
show $1\frac{1}{2}$ feet
above ground.
The supports for
the central par-
titions are stone
piers, 4 feet apart.
The Chimneys
are of hard brick
and mortar, pass-
ing through the
first story in two

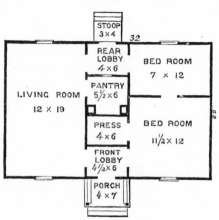

Fig. 4.—GROUND-PLAN OF HOUSE.

flues, but joined together beneath the roof, and finished
above as a single chimney. All the timber of the exterior
frame is of 4×6-inch spruce. The sills are laid flatways on the foundation, and the upright frame-work
stands upon them. The beams are of $1\frac{1}{4} \times 8$-inch spruce
planks ; they are notched 4 inches, to fit on the sill, and
bear on the foundation, and are nailed to the studding
and sills, binding the whole together. The ceiling-strips
are of $1\frac{1}{4} \times 5$-inch spruce, resting on the ties, and nailed
to the studding. The rafters are 2×4-inch wall-strips.
All beams, studding, and rafters, are placed 16 inches

apart from centers. The siding is of 10-inch dressed
pine. The roof is covered with 18-inch pine shingles,
laid on $1^1/_4 \times 2$-inch shingling-lath. The porch-frame is
of dressed and cornered timber, and is roofed with shingles on flooring laid face down. The flooring is $1^1/_8 \times 9$-
inch spruce "milled." The interior is plainly cased: for
doors and windows, $3^1/_4$ inches wide; base, 6 inches;

Fig. 5.—ELEVATION OF STORY-AND-A-HALF HOUSE.

chair-back in the living-room, 3 inches; all beveled. All
sashes and doors are $1^1/_4$ inch thick. The interior side-
walls and ceilings are white-sand finished, on brown mortar and seasoned lath. Many efforts have been made to
devise something cheaper than plastering for the inside
lining of walls, but no substitute has yet been found
to equal it in cheapness or durability. Plastering, as

usually prepared and applied, conduces to the healthfulness of any apartment, emits no odor of mouldiness, has
no attraction or harbor for vermin, is impervious to air,
and a non-conductor of sound.   Where linings of thin
wood or paper are used, it is necessary to deafen the partitions and ceilings, otherwise they will be noisy.   Sound
made in any one part will reverberate through the
house with drum-like suggestiveness.   Most of such materials absorb moisture rapidly from the atmosphere, and
when at any distance from the house-fires, so as not
to be warmed and dried, the moisture is retained in

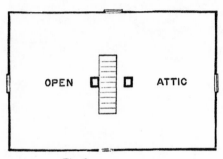

Fig. 6.—SECOND FLOOR.

them.   This is especially the case in chambers and closets.   Rather than seek a substitute for plastering, it is better to extend its use, and, where practicable, apply it as
an outside covering, as well as for inside linings, as described for Design VI.   The SECOND ELEVATION, (fig.
5,) shows an enlargement of the first, by increasing the
outlines of the roof, giving space for a SECOND FLOOR,
(fig. 6).   Such space, though not immediately required
for bedrooms, would be valuable for many purposes.
The appearance of the building is improved by the enlargement, and the extra cost will not exceed one hundred dollars.

Cost of Cottage—No. 1:

468 ft. stone foundation, at 5c. per foot	$23.40
1,000 bricks in chimneys, laid, at $12 per M	12.00
270 yards plastering, at 25c. per yard	67.50
576 feet of timber, at $15 per M	8.64

2 sills, 4×6 in. 80 ft. long.   2 plates, 4×6 in. 32 ft. long.
2 sills, 4×6 in. 32 ft. long.   4 posts, 4×6 in. 10 ft. long.
2 plates 4×6 in. 20 ft. long.   2 girts, 4×6 in. 20 ft. long.

160 wall-strips, at 13c. each	20.80
56 rough plank, at 16c. each	8.96
70 flooring. at 20c. each, $14; 115 siding, at 25c., $28.75	42.75
156 shingling-lath, at 6c. each	9.36
27 bunches shingles. at $1.50 each	40.50
Cornice and porch materials	21.00
4 windows, at $5 each. $20; 9 doors, at $3 each, $27	47.00
Closet finish and nails, $26.09; cartage, $12	38.09
Carpenter's labor, not included above	60.00
Painting	50.00
Total	$450.00

Extra cost of cottage—No. 2 :

3 windows, at $5 each. $15 ; 70 flooring, at 20c., $14	$29.00
25 siding, $6.25 ; 19 rough plank. $3.04	9.29
23 shingling-lath. $1.38 ; 4 bunches shingles, $6	7.38
25 wall-strips. $3.25 ; 400 brick, $4.80	8.05
Timber, $5 ; stairs, $20 ; porch, $5	30.00
Carpenter's labor	16.28
Total	$100.00

DESIGN III.

A COUNTRY COTTAGE, COSTING $550.

These plans are for a low-priced house, similar in character to those in Design II., but differing entirely in outlines and arrangement, and embracing a much larger area of floor space, with increased accommodations.... ELEVATION, (fig. 7.)—The Front is broken with angles, furnishing a greater number of vertical lines, thus giving relief from the depressing appearance that would otherwise be manifest. The roof projections are proportionate, with simple finish. The cornices of the central or main part are the most prominent, and have plain trusses. The gable openings supplying ventilation between the ceilings and roof.... GROUND-PLAN, (fig. 8).—The interior contains five quite ample rooms, conveniently arranged, besides a lobby, pantry, and two closets. Hight of ceilings in two principal rooms, $9^1/_2$ feet ; in the side extensions, 6 feet at the plate, following the rafters to

Fig. 7.—ELEVATION OF FRONT OF HOUSE.

the center of the rooms, and from thence are leveled across at the hight of 9 feet. The front entrance is through a lobby. (If desired to economize further, the front stoop and one door may be saved, by putting an arch in place of the front door, making a recessed porch of the lobby.) The Parlor has two front windows, and a closet, and adjoins the kitchen and two bedrooms. The Kitchen is large, has two windows, an open fire-place, and adjoins a commodious pantry, and a bedroom. The Pantry has a large window, and is shelved on one side and end. A convenient Clothes-press opens from the right-hand bedroom. The Chimney is near the center of the house, insuring much saving of heat. The interior of this house may be comfortably warmed from a single fire, by placing a Radiator in the parlor, and leading the fire-draught from the kitchen stove through it. As the peculiar form and construction of this radiator is comparatively new, having originated with me, a description is here given, which will enable any skillful sheet-iron worker to make one (see figs. 9 and 10) : *A*, is the parlor side of the chimney-breast ; *B*, the kitchen side ; *C*, chimney-flue ; *D*, kitchen fire-place, containing kitchen-stove ; *E*, smoke-pipe leading from the stove through the throat-piece, into the chim-

Fig. 8.—GROUND-PLAN.

ney-flue ; *F*, *F*, stove-pipe branches passing through the back of the fire-place, and connecting the smoke-pipe, *E*, with the radiator ; *G*, interior section of radiator ; *H*, face of radiator ; *I*, partition within radiator. The draught is regulated by a damper, *J*, in the smoke-pipe *E*, between the branches, *F*, *F*, and is forced through the radiator as required. The radiator may be made of any size desired to fit the mantle-opening, and if neatly constructed of Russian iron, will be quite ornamental.

The partition, *I*, is 5 inches wide, and extends to within
6 inches of the bottom at either side, has turned edges,
and is riveted to the front and back. In use, to start the
fire, a direct draught is made by opening the damper, *J*,
after which it may be closed to turn the draught through
the lower branch-pipe into the central part of the radiator, where it descends, passing the lower ends of the
partition, *I*, into the side passages, where it ascends and
enters the upper branch-pipe, leading to the smoke-pipe,
E. The bottom should have a collar to slide within the
upright part, to facilitate cleaning when necessary. If

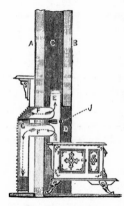

Fig. 9.—RADIATOR.

there is no hearth-stone to set the
radiator upon, the bottom may be
filled with an inch deep of coarse
plaster, which will make it safe
even on a carpet. In setting the
radiator, an inch or two of open
space should be left between it and
the chimney-back (just the thick-
ness of the interior wall-plates of
the mantle, against which the radiator should join.) Into the bottom
of this space, air may be introduced
from the outside of the house,
through a two-inch pipe. The air
thus let in becomes heated, and es-
capes around the margin, furnishing a pure healthful
supply to the room.... CONSTRUCTION.—The estimate
annexed, includes materials, and methods of construction
similar to those described for Design II. The form and
arrangement of this building admits of its being erected
in sections; the central or main part may be first put
up, and the side extensions added as means or necessity
requires or allow. In localities where it is difficult to get
dressed lumber, rough boards may be used for the siding,
put on vertically, and battened, but in this case it would

be practical to paint the cornices and other dressings only with lead and oil—using a lime-wash for the

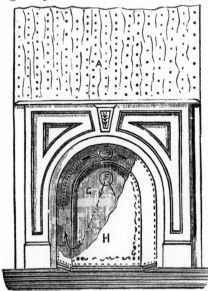

Fig. 10.—RADIATOR.

rough work. A durable wash may be made by slaking freshly-burned lump-lime in hot brine. This can be colored by adding dry-stainers as desired, and may be applied with an ordinary whitewash brush. Such work would greatly reduce the cost, and, if properly done, add a feature of rustic beauty, quite becoming in this class of building.

ESTIMATE cost of materials and labor :

340 ft. stone foundation, at 5c. per ft...	$17.00
1,000 bricks in chimneys, laid, at $12 per M	12.00
290 yards plastering, at 25c. per yard	72.50
800 ft. of timber, at $15 per M	12.00

2 sills, 4×6 in. 30 ft. long.	8 posts, 4×6 in. 13 ft. long.
2 sills, 4×6 in. 13 ft. long.	2 plates, 4×6 in. 30 ft. long.
2 sills, 4×6 in. 22 ft. long.	2 plates, 4×6 in. 13 ft. long.
4 sills, 4×6 in. 9 ft. long.	2 plates, 4×6 in. 22 ft. long.

300 wall-strips, at 13c. each	39.00
70 plank rough spruce, 1¼×10, at 16c. each	11.20
130 siding, dressed pine, ¾×10, at 25c. each	32.50
176 shingling-lath, at 6c. each	10.56
30 bunches shingles, at $1.50 per bunch	45.00
82 flooring, dressed spruce, at 20c. each	16.40
8 windows, at $5 each, $40 ; 10 doors, at $3 each, $30	70.00
Closet and base finish, $16: cornice materials, $15	31.00
Nails, $10 ; painting, $60 : cartage, $14	84.00
Carpenter's labor, $75 ; incidentals, $21.84	96.84
Total cost, complete	$550.00

DESIGN IV.

Fig. 11.—FRONT ELEVATION OF HOUSE.

A COUNTRY HOUSE, COSTING $550 TO $700.

This plan of a low-priced dwelling is adapted to the wants of many living in the country. It will accommodate a small family well, and has a pleasing appearance. .... EXTERIOR, (fig. 11.)—The Front has a sufficient variety of parts to insure a fair degree of picturesqueness. An allowable amount of neat tracery is admitted in the composition of the gables, and between the piazza columns, to give an expression of taste and cheerfulness. More than this would not accord with the utility and economy especially aimed at in these low-priced plans. If intended for a Summer Cottage, or Gate-lodge, for persons of larger means, the matter of exterior dress would assume quite a different aspect, and admit of

more liberal treatment.... GROUND-PLAN, (fig. 12.)—The
arrangement shown is adapted to an *eastward* frontage,
placing the Entrances and the Living-room on the pleasant side, where least exposed to northerly winds and cold.
Should an opposite frontage be selected, the plan may be
suited to it by reversing the sides, as this would be reflected if held
before a mirror.
The hight of
the ceilings are
10 feet. The
front entrances
open directly
from the piazza
to the parlor
and living-
room. These
entrances may
be protected
in winter by a
sash inclosure,
forming a pleas-
ant vestibule of
a part of the

Fig. 12.—PLAN OF FIRST FLOOR.

piazza. The principal rooms are a Parlor, Kitchen, and
two Bedrooms. The Parlor is in front of the main building, and of sufficient size for the ordinary uses of such an
apartment. The Kitchen is intended as the Living-
room, where the family, maintaining the simplicity of
cottage life, spend much of their in-door time, sharing
together the domestic cares and comforts. It is sufficiently spacious to admit of the requisite furniture, and
allow of the ordinary family gathering without crowding.
It has three windows; if desired, the upper part of the
front door may have sashes, giving views in three directions. The pantry and lobby, at the rear, are of equal

size, both opening from the kitchen. The two Bedrooms adjoin each other (but have no communication between them in the plan. This may be arranged as desired.) One opens from the parlor, the other from the kitchen, and each has a closet. The Chimney is placed between the kitchen and parlor, with an open fire-place on the kitchen side. The method of heating, described for Design III., would insure the comfortable warming of both

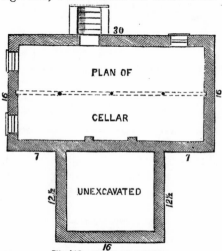

PLAN OF

CELLAR

UNEXCAVATED

Fig. 13.—PLAN OF CELLAR.

of the principal rooms from one kitchen fire... CELLAR, (fig. 13.)—Hight, 6½ feet. The dimensions embrace the space below the kitchen and the bedrooms ; it has three windows and an outside entrance. The part under the parlor is unexcavated.... CONSTRUCTION.—The Foundation-walls are of broken stone and mortar, and show 2 feet above ground. Those under the parlor are laid in trenches, extending below the reach of frost. The chimney is of hard brick and mortar. The frame-work, roofing, and exterior plastering, are similar to those described for Design VI. The gables are inclosed with vertical boarding, having their lower ends cut to pattern, and are battened over the joints. The ornamental verges in the gable-cornices are of pine boards, and, being of simple design, are readily made, and put in position while building. A pleasing effect is produced by "lining off" the surface of the exterior plastering into courses or squares. This is easily done with a "straight-edge," and an **S** shaped iron while finishing. The final "Stearate" covering (see Design VI.) may be divided and shaded in two parts, and so applied as to give the alternate squares slight changes of shade. The best results may be obtained from *exterior plastering* where properly done. It is impervious to either air or water, and therefore equals the more expensive methods of inclosures for houses of this character. It should not be attempted over *horizontal* lines of framework, as the shrinking and consequent contraction will cause a bulging and cracking of the plaster at those points. Whenever obliged to cross such timbers, the upright framework must be halved on to them, and continued in whole lengths, to prevent such contractions. All joinings with the exterior wood-finish must be carefully made, especially at the top, to prevent water from entering, and running down behind the walls. Wide projectives of cornices afford a valuable protection for such walls against driving storms. Exterior plastering may be done in any season that is free from frost. An ordinary rain will do no injury to either of the two coats of plaster after they have become "set." The "Stearate" should be applied as soon as the plastering is thoroughly dried.

ESTIMATE for cost of materials and labor :

54 yards excavation, at 20c. per yard	$10.80
1,300 ft. foundation, at 10½c. per ft	136.50
1,250 brick, laid, at $12 per M	15.00
28 ft. stone steps and sills, at 28c. per ft:	7.84
120 yards exterior plastering, at 30c. per yard	36.00
224 " interior " " 25c. " "	56.00
1.700 ft. of timber, at $15 per M	25.50

2 sills, 3×8 in. 30 ft. l'ng | 3 plates, 4×6 in. 16 ft. long | 7 beams, 3×8 in. 13 ft. long
3 sills, 3×8 in. 16 ft. l'ng | 2 plates. 4×6 in. 13 ft. long | 10 beams, 2×8 in. 16 ft. long
2 sills, 3×8 in. 13 ft. l'ng | 9 posts, 4×6 in. 10 ft. long | 7 beams. 2×8 in. 13 ft. long
2 plates.4×6 in. 30 ft. l'g | 14 beams,3×8 in. 13 ft. l'ng | 1 piazza. 2×8 in. 18 ft. long

200 wall-strips, at 10c. each. $20 : cornice materials and gable finish, $18.25	38 25
180 shingling-lath, at 5c. each. $9.00 ; 16 spruce-planks, at 20c. each, $3.20.	12.20
34 bunches shingles. at $1.25 per bunch	42.50
80 flooring-planks, at 20c.. $16 : piazza, $40	56.00
3 cellar-windows, $9 ; 8 plain windows, $56.	65.00
11 doors. $44 : closet-finish. $12 : nails. $10 : carting. $12	78.00
Painting, $30 ; carpenter's labor, $75 ; incidentals, $15.41	120.41
Total cost	$700.00
If cellar is omitted, deduct, $167.14. Cost without cellar	$532.86

2

DESIGN V.

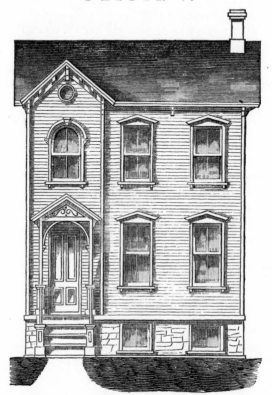

Fig. 14.—FRONT ELEVATION.—Scale, 8 feet to 1 inch.

A CONVENIENT HOUSE, COSTING $650.

The accompanying plans were designed for a simple, compact, and economical house, and will be appreciated by any one who may desire to know just how little is required to build a comfortable home. They provide ample room for a small family.... The CELLAR extends under the whole house, the walls are built as shown in the details of foundation and frame, given in Design VI., with 3 feet of masonry and 3 feet of frame-work.... The FIRST STORY contains a good-sized Hall, Parlor, and Kitchen, or Living-room, with two closets, pump, and sink. The stairs to the cellar lead directly from the kitchen, passing down under the stairs in the main hall. A "fire-place heater" can be put in the parlor fire-place, which will also warm the chamber above. This method of of heating is economical, and occupies but little room...... The SECOND STORY has three good-sized rooms, two closets, and small hall, in the main house, and an attic over the kitchen. The floor of the attic is one foot lower than that of the main house; this

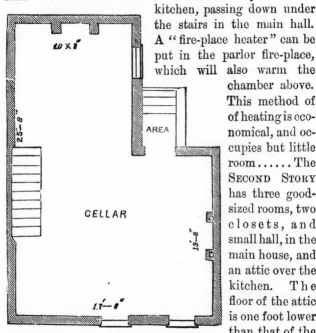

Fig. 15.—CELLAR.—Scale, 8 feet to 1 inch.

gives valuable room for storage, etc.... The hight of the first story of the main house is 8 feet 6 inches ; of the second story, 7 feet. The hight of the kitchen ceiling is 7¹/₂ feet. The attic is arranged to have just standing room in the center.... A great saving of time and trouble is made, when openings are provided for *regular sizes* of sash, blinds, and doors, as they may be obtained of seasoned and well-made stock, at any time, from any

dealer in such materials. These plans are drawn with
reference to such regular sizes, viz. : the first-story windows are 2 ft. 7 in. × 5 ft. 6 in. ; second story, 2 ft. 7
in. × 4 ft. 6 in. ; cellar, 2 ft. × 2 ft. 8 in., all $1^{1}/_{4}$ inch
thick. All principal windows
should have their frames made
with pockets and pulleys, and
the sash hung with iron
weights and good cord. The
cost for the addition of these
necessary parts,
beyond what is
required for the
plain frame, is
about as follows,
for each window
of ordinary size:
4 pulleys, (at
40c. per doz.)
14c. ; 20 lbs. iron
weights, $2^{1}/_{2}$c.
per lb., 50c. ;
$^{1}/_{2}$ lb. sash-cord,
16c. per lb., 8c. ;
1 doz. screws,
$^{7}/_{8}$ in., 35c. per
gross, 3c. ; la-
bor putting in
pockets, pul-

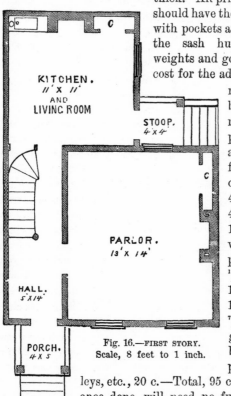

Fig. 16.—FIRST STORY.
Scale, 8 feet to 1 inch.

leys, etc., 20 c.—Total, 95 cents, and when
once done, will need no further attention
or expense, while the house lasts. The
satisfaction of having neat-fitting, easy-working sash,
where the upper, or lower one, may be opened at will, is
great. The saving of little fingers, and older nerves, to
say nothing of shattered sash and glass, more than repays

the extra cost of hanging sash .... The front, rear, and parlor DOORS are 2 ft. 8 in. × 6 ft. 8 in. × 1½ in.; other first-story doors, 2 ft. 6 in. × 6 ft. 8 in. × 1¼ in.; second-story doors, 3 ft. 6 in. × 6 ft. 6 in. × 1¼ in.; all 4-paneled, and neatly moulded. The 1½-inch doors have mortise-locks; other doors rim-locks, all with porcelain knobs and escutcheons .... BLINDS are included for the first and second stories, in the estimate appended, at an average cost of $2.40 per pair, and may be omitted, but are recommended as useful; they protect the sash from storms, and can be operated to give almost any desired light or shade in the rooms .....
Many people may be in circumstances that would justify the building of one part of a house first, to be occupied as a temporary residence until means and opportunity warrant the building of the whole. A

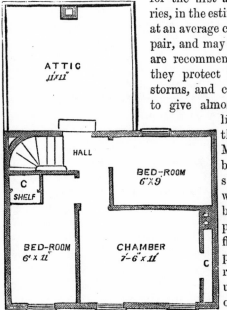

Fig. 17.—SECOND STORY.—Scale, 8 feet to 1 inch.

newly-married couple could arrange to have the kitchen part built as a residence for a season, rather than forego the opportunity of setting out trees, vines, and shrubbery, planting, and otherwise developing their grounds. They would then be near the work when building the main part, to superintend it, and care for materials, saving much that is often wasted, or lost. The wing, or kitchen part, could be built at a cost of about $185, so arranged as that the main house could be joined to it at at any time—or, what would be better, the main house may be built first, at a cost of about $650, and the kitchen added at convenience . . . . The exterior dressing of cornice, window-caps, and stoop, are decided in their character for simplicity and boldness, giving a generous and finished appearance to the whole. . . . NOVELTY SIDING, fig. 18, is mentioned in many of the estimates for these houses. This form of siding I first introduced some sixteen years ago, since which time it has grown into general favor and use in this neighborhood. It has the following merits to recommend it : 1st, It is easily put on by ordinary mechanics. 2d, When properly nailed to the frame, it strengthens it, so as to make bracing of the frame almost unnecessary. 3d, The spaces between the studding, when the interior is plastered, are each air-tight compartments, containing only stationary air, which is a non-conductor of cold (or heat), thus protecting the inside wall from the extreme changes of outward temperature. 4th, A cheaper quality of lumber can be used, the more cross-grained the materials, the less likely they are to check, or shrink, and any small, sound knots are easily covered with shellac before painting, which closes them effectually. 5th, The general surface is even, so that any brackets or other ornamentation can be put on without the trouble and difficulty of "scribing" them up to the clap-boarding. . . . The SHINGLING referred to in the estimate is of 18-inch pine shingles, and may be laid $5^3/_4$ inch to the weather, and secured with large-headed "shingle-nails." It is best in laying shingles to lap at one-third the breadth, never in the center, for should one shingle check in the center, as they are liable to do, an opening is made through the

Fig. 18.—"NOVELTY SIDING."

three courses, and a leaky roof will be the result. "Shingling-lath" $1^{1}/_{4} \times 2$ in., with the lower edge placed just where the buts of the shingles would cover, will allow air to freely circulate on both sides of the shingles, and preserve them one-third longer than when laid on close planking, which holds the moisture, and assists decay of every part of the roof.... GUTTERS.—The old wooden gutter has nearly gone into disuse, and always seemed a barrier to any satisfactory finish of cornice. It was difficult to get timber of sufficient width for projections, and in such cases, the cornices were proportioned by boxing off, and building up around this "gutter-stick," which was bad construction—the outer-edge of the gutter, being higher than the edge next the house, would cause the water, during heavy storms, or when

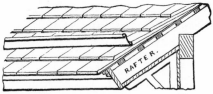

the leader was choked up, to flow over against the frame-work of the building, which was one of the most fre-quent causes of

Fig. 19.—PORTION OF ROOF AND GUTTER.

decay and settling in the older houses in this country.—The tin-lined "box" and "trough" gutters are often troublesome ; the tin can not be laid in them except in long lengths, which have been soldered together while flat and smooth. To lay these long lengths into the ready-formed gutter, requires much bending and ham-mering, which breaks the best tin at the soldered joints, on the under-side, where it is impossible to repair it, so that, while it may not appear at once to leak, it is sure to do so soon, to be discovered after the cornice has been swelled out of shape or destroyed. The gutter that I have adopted in all cases where practicable (see section, fig. 19), either for shingles or slate, is made of charcoal-tin, 14 inches wide, in lengths as long as can be well handled. One edge is turned or rolled up around a $^6/_8$ iron rod, which makes a strong edge. Then a bend is made at $3^1/_2$ inches from the turned edge, forming a right angle the whole length. This is laid on the second course of shingles, with one end lower than the other, so as to give a good run for the water. The ends are turned up, where required, to stop the water, and a tube put through the cornice in the usual manner.... For TIN ROOFS, having a pitch of at least one inch to the foot, the gutters are formed in a similar manner, with the flat, or bottom part, about $^1/_2$ inch wide, making a flange, which is soldered to the roof near the eaves, to a line drawn at an angle to make one end lower than the other, as for shingle roofs. This is the simplest and best kind of gutter, will outlast any other, and in the event of a possible damage, or leakage, no harm will be done beyond the loss or waste of the water that runs off over the eaves. It can be easily repaired, or replaced at any time, without interfering with the principal roof, and it saves the trouble and expense of building and boxing for gutters, or of making cornices with special reference to them, and it is cheaply constructed.—ESTIMATE OF COST of building by this plan in the vicinity of New York City :

38 yards excavation, at 20c. per yard...............................	$7.60
5,000 brick, furnished and laid, at $12 per M.........................	60.00
230 yards lath and plastering, 3 coats, at 28c. per yard..............	64.40
1,412 ft. timber, at $15 per M......................................	21.18

1 sill, 3×8 in. 92 ft. long.	1 girt, 4×8 in. 12 ft. long.
4 posts, 4×6 in. 21 ft. long.	2 ties, 4×6 in. 16 ft. long.
2 plates, 4×6 in. 19 ft. long.	2 ties, 4×6 in. 19 ft. long.
2 plates, 4×6 in. 12 ft. long.	18 beams, 3×8 in. 16 ft. long.
10 beams. 3×7 in. 12 ft. long.	

1 locust-post, 4 inch......................................	35
220 wall-strips. 2×4 in. 13 ft. long. at 10c......................	22.00
160 novelty siding-boards, 9½ in., at 28c.........................	44.80
30 rabbeted siding, 9½ in., at 28c., $8.40 ; 92 ft. cornice materials, $15...	23.40
100 shingling-lath, at 6c., $6 ; 16 bunches shingles, at $1.50, $24........	30.00
Tin gutters and leaders	7.00
90 tongued and grooved flooring. 9¼ in., at 30c......................	27.00
8 windows with blinds, at $8, $64 ; 3 cellar windows, plain, at $3, $9..	73.00
2 stoop materials. $20 ; stairs, 1st story and cellar, $40..............	60.00
12 doors and materials.......................................	48.00
Carpenter's labor (not included above)...........................	75.00
Painting. two coats, $40 ; cartage. average one mile, $12...........	52.00
Extras, for base, sink. pump, and nails, etc......................	34.27
Total cost of materials and construction........................	$650.00

DESIGN VI.

Fig. 20.—ELEVATION OF HOUSE.—Scale, 8 feet to 1 inch.

A HOUSE COSTING $700.

The plans here given are of simple design, intended to meet the large and increasing demand for low-priced country or village houses, having at the same time some architectural beauty. Without this latter feature, a comfortable house of this size can, in many places, be erected

for much less than $700 even.... The house here de-
scribed provides for as much room as a small family
would require, while at the same time it admits of future
enlargement, as one's necessity or means may indicate, by

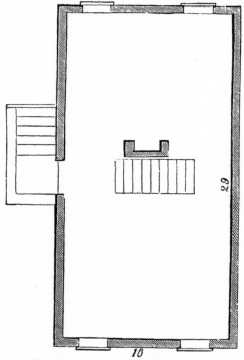

Fig. 21.—CELLAR.—Scale, 8 feet to 1 inch.

additions, ells, or wings, at either side, or rear. In all
cases, when planning small houses, it is best to provide
for such enlargements. The triplet window in front is
so arranged that it can be readily changed to a bay-window, when that improvement can be afforded, without
marring the rest of the wood-work, or the harmony of
the front elevation.... The Cornice of the main building

is bracketed, and projects sufficient to relieve it of the
stunted look so common to country houses.   The brackets are made of 2×4-inch timber, in three pieces each,
mitred to the angles required, and nailed together (see

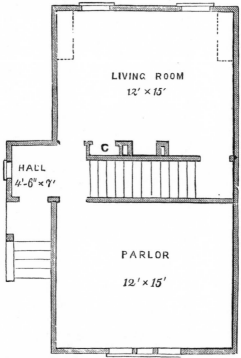

Fig. 22.—FIRST STORY.—Scale, 8 feet to 1 inch.

fig. 25), making an effective support and pleasant appearance.... A large saving in expense of foundations is
secured by the following method of construction (see
section of foundation and frame, fig. 24).   The excavation is made for the cellar $2\frac{1}{2}$ feet deep.   A foundation
of 8-inch brick-work, 3 feet high, or 6 inches above the
level of the ground only, is required.   A sill of 3×8-inch

timber is laid on, and "flush" with the inside of the wall, to provide nailing for the wainscoting of the basement, if it is afterwards finished off.... The beams or joists for the first floor are supported by a plank-strip five

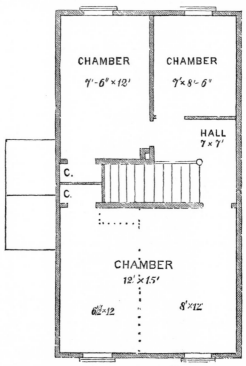

CHAMBER
7'-6" × 12'

CHAMBER
7' × 8'- 6"

HALL
7 × 7'

C.

C.

CHAMBER
12' × 15'

6½ × 12

8' × 12'

Fig. 23.—SECOND STORY.—Scale, 8 feet to 1 inch.

inches wide, let into the inside of the frame at a proper hight, and securely fastened with heavy nails. The other parts of the framing are executed, and the whole raised, in the usual manner.... The inclosing, or siding, below the first story, is of 10-inch boards rabbeted and cross-grooved in imitation of large stone-work, and painted in contrast with the principal body of the house, and the water-table is put just above them.... Many small houses in the country are built without any permanent foundation, but are temporarily supported on posts set in the ground, and "boarded down." They are always shaky, and doubtful while they stand, and are frequently blown over altogether. As will be readily seen, the above method provides for the saving of one-half of the mason-work in the foundation. In many places stone is abundant, and will answer the same purpose as brick in this case, except for the 6 inches above ground. The laying up of a single-face wall, $2\frac{1}{2}$ feet high, of rough stone and mortar, would cost but a trifle. If the cellar should be finished at any time for basement purposes, these walls would be much drier and more healthful than when the walls are entirely of masonry. In this case it would be preferable to have the foundation walls 6 inches higher, so as to have the basement rooms 7 feet in the clear.... Several houses have been built on this plan in villages, and in most cases it has been decided not to have any rear outside door for the first story (fig. 22), but to wait until a kitchen could be finished in the front part of the cellar, when the common entrance would be by the area to the kitchen. In the plan (fig. 22), we have indicated two rear windows, but a door may take the place of either of them. We have also indicated by dotted lines where pantry, sink, etc., may be placed in the corner, according to the wishes of the proprietor.... There is but one chimney. The parlor is heated by running a stove-pipe

Fig. 24.

through earthen thimbles placed in the partitions under the stairs, to the chimney, which is perfectly safe, and no heat is lost. When desired, a fire-place, or stove-pipe flue, may be carried up through the parlor, as well as through the living-room, and the two be brought to-

gether above the stairs into one chimney. .... The SECOND STORY, (fig. 23), may be divided into three rooms, the front one being 12×15 feet ; or, if preferred, this front room may be divided into two smaller rooms, as indicated by the dotted lines. One may be 8×12, and the other $6^1/_2 \times 12$. The latter would be large enough for an ordinary bed ($4^1/_2 \times 6^1/_2$ feet), with stand or chair by the window ; and in this case a small closet could be cut off from the corner, opening into the large room, as shown by the dotted lines.

Fig. 25.

COST.—The following estimate in detail, at present prices, near this city, will enable any one to determine the cost of building by this plan. Allowance can be made for any difference in cost of materials or labor as required in other localities :

43 yards excavation, at 20c. per yard	$8.60
6,000 brick, laid complete, at $12 per M	72.00
1,636 ft. timber, at $15 per M	24.50

2 sills, 3×8 in. 29 ft. long.	2 sills, 3×3 in. 16 ft. long.
4 posts, 4×7 in. 21 ft. long.	28 beams, 3×8 in. 16 ft. long.
2 ties, 4×6 in. 29 ft. long.	2 plates, 4×6 in. 29 ft. long.
2 ties, 4×6 in. 16 ft. long.	2 plates, 4×6 in. 16 ft. long.

32 rafters, 3×4 in. 12 ft. long, at 20c	6.40
200 wall-strips, 2×4 in. 13 ft. long. at 11c	22.00
162 novelty siding-boards, 9½ in., at 28c	45.36
28 rabbeted siding, 10 in., at 28c	7.84
97 flooring spruce, 9½ in., at 28c	27.16
123 shingling-lath, 1¼×2 in., at 6c	7.38
22 bunches shingles, 18 in., at $1.25	27.50
14 windows, with blinds, two stories, 9 at $8 ; 5 at $3	87.00
2 stairs, $25 ; 11 doors and trimmings, $44 ; 1 stoop materials, $10	79.00
14 rough spruce-plank, 1¼×10 in., at 30c	4.20
100 feet cornice materials	20.00
Carpenter's labor (not included above)	90.00
350 yards plastering, three coats, at 25c	87.50
Cartage, average one mile	12.00
Painting, two coats, $40 ; extras, for tin, nails, etc. $31.56	71.56
Total cost in above style	$700.00

DESIGN VII.

Fig. 26.—ELEVATION OF FRONT OF HOUSE.

COUNTRY HOUSE, COSTING $750 TO $1,050.

These plans represent a commodious dwelling house, constructed with especial regard for economy and utility, and they will be appreciated by those desiring to provide a comfortable, permanent shelter for home by the use of limited means.... ELEVATION, fig 26).—In preparing plans for "low-priced" houses, the simplest outlines are indicated. Having to combine usefulness and small outlay, there can be no latitude for architectural display, beyond mere matters of accommodation and complete-

ness. The exterior of this example fairly expresses its
domestic purpose. The breadth of the front, the preponderance of horizontal lines, and the hooded roof, are each
indicative of strength, and suggest its adaptation to rural
situations. The satisfactory appearance of this house
will greatly depend on its location. The best results
would be obtained by placing it on a slight knoll, giving
it additional altitude. This would prevent its being ob-
scured by shrub-
bery and trees,
which are indis-
pensable accom-
paniments of a
properly devel-
oped homestead
.... CEL-
LAR, (fig. 27).—
Hight, $6\frac{1}{2}$ feet.
It has three win-
dows, an outside
entrance, and
stairway leading
to the kitchen

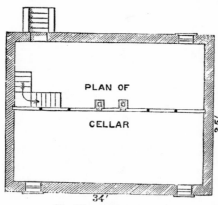

Fig. 27.—PLAN OF CELLAR.

above .... FIRST STORY, (fig. 28.)—Hight of ceiling, 10
feet. The accommodations, consisting of five rooms, a
pantry, and two closets, are adapted to a good-sized family. The Parlor and Kitchen are the principal rooms,
and occupy the middle portion, their sides being protected by other rooms, and, having the fire-place between
them, they are easily warmed. The device for heating
described for Design III. would serve admirably in this
house. Two Bedrooms adjoin the parlor. Many might
choose to have *double* doors entering these bedrooms, to
allow all three rooms to be used together occasionally.
This would not preclude the use of the smaller ones as
bedrooms, or, if preferred, as a sewing-room and a library.

The Kitchen is the largest apartment, and has doors leading to the pantry, bedroom, parlor, stairway, and the rear entrance. The outside or entrance doors may be protected in severe seasons by storm-doors hung to open outward, with loose joint-buts to allow of their ready removal. The rear veranda is similar to the front one shown on the elevation..... SECOND STORY, (fig. 29).—The front portion only is finished, with ceilings 8 feet high, and is divided into two chambers and four closets. The rear portion is left unfinished, to be used as an open garret. The space above the ceiling of the finished portion may be floored

Fig. 28.—PLAN OF FIRST FLOOR.

over with boards, to serve for storage of quilting-frames, trunks, etc.... CONSTRUCTION.—The excavations for the cellar are 4 feet deep. The foundation-walls are of broken stone, laid in mortar, and show 2 feet above the earth-grade. A strong girder, resting on large posts, or columns of stone or brick, supports the center of the building. In setting the girder, it should be elevated from $1/2$ to $3/4$ of an inch in the center, rising gradually from each end, to allow for settling, which invariably occurs from shrinkage of the interior frame-work. The timber for the frame-work is indicated in the estimates

below, and is substantially framed together. All the outside studding is *halved* over the principal timbers, to prevent vertical shrinkage from affecting the exterior covering of the side-walls. The exterior covering is of lath
and plaster, as follows: all cornices and other dressings,
and the roof, should first be completed—and all window
and door frames set and cased. The outside frame
should then be thoroughly lathed outside and inside.
All this is to prevent jarring or pounding on these parts
during the appli-
cation or setting
of the plaster.

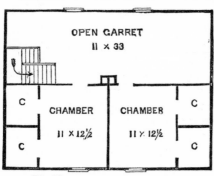

Fig. 29.—PLAN OF SECOND FLOOR.

The plaster is
made in the usual
manner of fresh
lime and sharp
sand, with half a
bushel of hair to
each barrel of
lime used, and al-
lowed to lay two
weeks to insure
a thorough slaking and permeation of the lime. It is
then applied in two coats—the first a "scratch," the
second a "browning." The surface is floated with a
darby, (not trowelled). After having stood a sufficient
time to become dry, the whole is covered with a preparation called "Stearate of Lime," using an ordinary whitewash brush. The formula for making this stearate of
lime (known only to a few, who have treated it as a secret,)
is here published for the first time, and it will be under-
stood by those familiar with the nature and operation of
slaking lime. The ingredients are simply fresh-burned
finishing-lime, using the lumps only, unrendered beef-
suet, and hot water. It is necessary that these parts be
kept in lively motion while dissolving, or they will be

entirely destroyed by "burning." The usual process is to sink a large barrel, having an open end, 2 feet in the ground, pounding the earth around to make it firm. An upright piece, 4 inches in diameter, and 6 feet long, is set upright in the center of the barrel, and held in position by cleats at the bottom and top, leaving the upright free to turn. Arms are put through the upright within the barrel, and a cross-bar or lever is attached to the upper end—the whole making an apparatus similar to a "clay-mill." One bushel of lime, 20 lbs. of suet (chopped fine), and a barrel of boiling water are provided ; and while one works the "mill," another feeds alternately lime, suet, and hot water. This quantity of material, costing about $2, will make a full barrel of the preparation. Any desired shade may be afterwards given by adding stainers. This mixture is applied while hot—two coats being necessary to insure a thorough covering. This will also be found a valuable preparation for covering exterior brick or concrete work. It is impervious to water, and will outlast any of the paints prepared for such purpose. All other information concerning the finish of this house may be inferred upon a careful study of the following estimates.—ESTIMATE cost of materials and labor :

95 yards excavation, at 20c. per yard	$19.00
1,062 ft. stone-foundation, at 15c. per ft.	159.30
24 ft. stone steps and coping, at 28c. per ft.	6.72
2,000 bricks in chimneys, laid, at $12 per M.	24.00
517 yards plastering, inside. at 25c. per yard	129.25
130 " " outside. at 30c. per yard	39.00
1,850 ft. of timber, at $15 per M	27.75

2 sills, 3×8 in. 34 ft. long.	2 plates, 4×6 in. 15 ft. long.
2 sills, 3×8 in. 25 ft. long.	2 perlines, 3×8 in. 25 ft. long.
1 girder, 4×8 in. 32 ft. long.	2 perlines. 4×6 in. 18 ft. long.
4 posts, 4×8 in. 11 ft. long.	100 beams, 1¼×8 in. 13 ft. long.
3 ties, 3×6 in. 34 ft. long.	

300 wall-strips, at 11c. each	33.00
4 locust-posts. at 30c. each, $1.20 ; 190 flooring. at 20c. each, $38....	39.20
216 shingling-lath. at 6c. each	12.96
39 bunches shingles, at $1.25 per bunch	48.75
3 cellar windows, at $3, $9 ; 12 plain windows, at $7, $84	93.00
17 doors. at $4 each, $68 ; 2 verandas, $50 each, $100	168.00
Stairs, $20 ; cornice materials, $18	38.00
Closet finish and base, $15 ; nails, $12 ; cartage, $20	47.00
Painting, $40 ; carpenter's labor, $100 ; incidentals, $25.07	165.07
Total cost, complete	$1,050.00
Omitting cellar and verandas would save	300.00
Total, after deductions	**$750.00**

DESIGN VIII.

Fig. 30.—FRONT ELEVATION.

A COTTAGE, COSTING $800 TO $1,050.

This design is an enlargement of the small cottage described in Design I. The arrangements are very complete in convenience, appearance, and economy.... Ex-

TERIOR, (fig. 30).—The outlines and style are simple. The front is enlivened by the Porch, Bay-Window, and other projections. The details of finish are of neat de-

sign, and in harmony, giving an agreeable expression of taste and refinement — features especially pleasing in cottage architecture. .... CELLAR, (fig. 31). — Hight in clear, $6^1/_2$ feet. It is under the main building only ; has two windows, and stairs leading to the first story. It contains 378 feet area, giving abundant room for all ordinary requirements...... FIRST STORY, (fig. 32). — Hight of ceiling, 9 feet. The best use is made of the space by having but few divisions, leaving good-sized rooms.

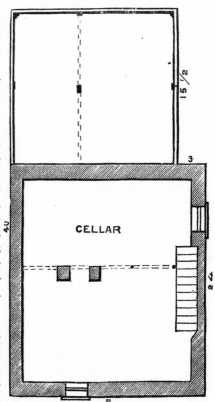

Fig. 31.—PLAN OF CELLAR.

The Hall is small, but is conveniently arranged to answer all necessary purposes. It is entered from the front porch, and communicates directly with the parlor and dining-room, and by the main stairs with the second story. There is sufficient room for a hat-rack

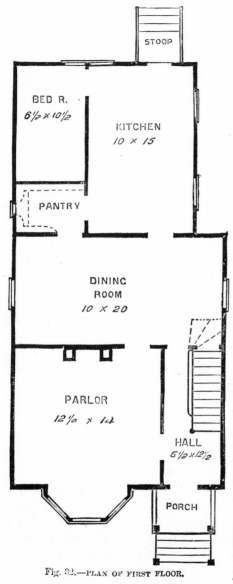

Fig. 32.—PLAN OF FIRST FLOOR.

at the right of the front door. The Parlor is of fair size, the large bay-window adding materially to its area and cheerfulness. With very little expense in furniture, this apartment may be made pleasant and cosey. The Dining-room extends the whole width of the house, and has a window at each end. It is conveniently arranged, with doors opening from the hall, parlor, kitchen, pantry, and to the stairs. The Kitchen is commodious and pleasant; has three windows, an outside rear entrance, and adjoins the din-

ing-room, pantry, and bedroom. The Pantry is sufficiently large and convenient to answer the requirements
of both dining-room and kitchen. It has a small window, and is thoroughly shelved. The Bedroom opens
directly from the kitchen. Its purpose in the partial
erection (as shown in Design I.) may be changed in the
completed building here described by making it an

auxiliary of the
kitchen for the
coarser work ;
or, if needed,
it may still be
be used as a
bedroom for
help..... SEC-
OND STORY,
(fig. 33).—
Hight of ceil-
ing, 8 feet.
There is a hall,
two chambers,
two bedrooms,
and two closets,
in this story,
and no waste
room. The
Hall is just

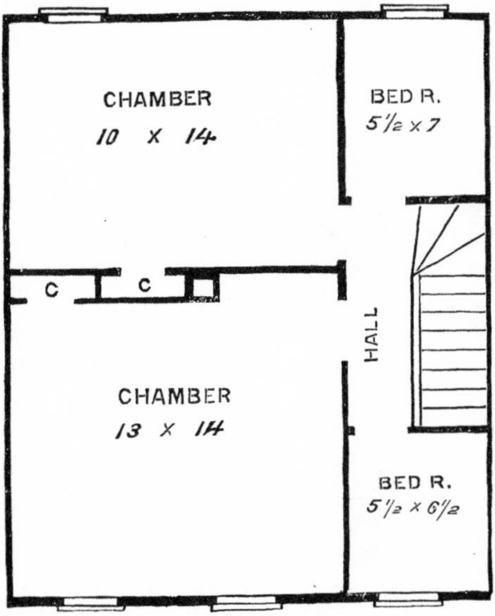

Fig. 33.—PLAN OF SECOND FLOOR.

large enough for convenience. The Chambers are of
ample dimensions, with a chimney between them, admitting the use of stoves when required.... CONSTRUC-
TION.—The Foundations for the main house are of broken
stone and mortar, showing three feet above ground,
neatly pointed where exposed to sight. The Wing is
supported on piers, as described in Design I. Girders
(shown on the cellar-plan by dotted lines), supported on
strong posts, carry the central portions of the building.

The shortness of the spans between bearings allow very light floor-beams. It is, however, important that the beams should be *bridged* to secure uniformity of strength, and prevent vibrations. The Frame is constructed in the usual manner—all the ties, girts, and headers being "framed in." The inclosing is sufficiently indicated in the estimate. The front windows have semi-circular heads outside. In their construction the frames and sash are square, to admit ordinary curtain fixtures on the inside. The circular head is outside of, and "planted" on the flat casing, or "blind-strip," and is made perfectly tight by a flange of tin. The additional expense of such circular finish is but trifling, compared with its good appearance. The side and rear windows have square heads, with rabbeted drips. Blinds are intended for all windows above the cellar. Ventilators are placed in each gable. The Porch has boxed pedestals and columns, scroll-sawed balusters, and circular spandrells. The inside walls and ceilings are "sand-finished" on two coats of brown mortar. The main stairs are constructed with a quarter circle, and winders at the top. These winders extend beyond the hall into the ceilings of the dining-room (as sketched), but do not interfere with its use, or seriously injure its appearance. The Bay-Window is neatly arched on the inside. Marble mantels are put in the parlor and dining-room, and shelves in the chambers. The second story-hall is lighted through the door (sash) of the front bedroom.... SUGGESTIONS.—This plan was arranged to suit a village lot 25 feet in width, leaving a passage-way at the side. This necessitated placing the wing at the rear of the main house. If there is more ground, the wing may be placed at the right of the main part, facing the road. The communications between the dining-room and wing would be still similar to those shown. The window at the right of the dining-room would be placed in the rear. These changes entail no extra expense, if

determined on before commencing to build.—ESTIMATE
cost of materials and labor for main house :

56 yards excavation, at 20c. per yard	$11.20
875 ft. stone-foundation. at 5c. per ft	43.75
2,000 brick, furnished and laid, at $12 per M	24.00
340 yards plastering. complete, at 25c. per yard	85.00
1,126 ft. of timber, at $15 per M	16.89

2 sills, 4×6 in. 24 ft. long.	4 posts, 4×6 in. 19 ft. long.
2 sills. 4×6 in. 21 ft. long.	2 plates. 4×6 in. 24 ft. long.
9 ties, 4×6 in. 24 ft. long.	1 girder, 4×6 in. 21 ft. long.
4 ties, 4×6 in. 21 ft. long.	22 beams, 3×6 in. 24 ft. long.

250 wall-strips, at 11c. each	27.50
162 siding, 9 in., at 20c. each	32.40
Cornice materials	18.00
135 shingling-lath, at 5c. each	6.75
8 rough planks, at 20c. each	1.60
24 bunches shingles, at $1.25 per bunch	30.00
112 flooring. 9 in., at 25c	28 00
2 cellar windows. complete, at $4	8.00
1 bay-window, complete	40.00
5 plain windows, complete, at $12	60.00
Stairs, complete, $40; 12 doors, complete, $96	136.00
Mantels, $39.91 ; porch. $30 ; closets, $10	79.91
Nails, $9 ; painting. $50; carting, $12	71.00
Carpenter's labor (not included above)	80.00
Total cost of main house	$800.00
Add Design I.'s estimate for wing	250.00
Total for whole complete	$1,050.00

DESIGN IX.

COUNTRY OR VILLAGE COTTAGE, COSTING $1,000.

This plan is designed to answer many requests for a
" cosey and homelike Cottage, suited to the wants of
Mechanics and Laboring People, costing from $700 to
$1,000." It is best adapted to a westward frontage—
with the hall, entrances, and porches protected from the
north, but may be easily adapted to an opposite frontage
by reversing the plan—placing the hall, etc., on the opposite side of the main house. The width, 21 feet,
adapts it to a 25-foot village lot, leaving a side passage to
the rear.... EXTERIOR, (figs. 34 and 35.)—The *style* of
any building is determined by the form of its roof ; the
steep and hooded style in this design accords fully with
domestic feelings and artistic sentiments, and is growing

3

Fig. 34.—FRONT VIEW OF COTTAGE.

in public favor for suburban structures. Compared with the usual *Mansard* style is more practical, less expensive, and serves equally well. The side-angles, porches, bay-window, cornices, and chimneys, each of simple construction, make up a pleasing variety of parts. All superfluous ornamentation is avoided. A too common fault prevails in villages, and even in the country, of building close up to the street lines. A clear depth of at least 20 feet in front should be devoted to a flower-garden, shrubbery, and vines, for flowers are proper accessories of cottage adornment, and architectural ornamentation can never compensate for their

Fig. 35.—SIDE VIEW OF COTTAGE.

absence.... CELLAR, (fig 36.)—Hight of ceiling, $6\frac{1}{2}$ feet.
It extends under the front half of the building, giving an
average area of $11\frac{1}{2} \times 15$ feet—quite sufficient for ordinary requirements. It has two small front windows. A
good ventilation may be had through the chimney ; openings in the rear foundation allow a circulation of air over
the unexcavated portion.... FIRST STORY, (fig. 37.)—
Hight of ceiling, 9
feet ; is divided in-
to a hall, parlor,
living - room, rear
entry, and a closet.
The Hall, entered
from the front
porch, connects
through doors with
the parlor, living-
room, and rear en-
try, and contains
the main stairs.
The Parlor has a
large bay-window
in the front, oppo-
site to which is a
marble shelf rest-
ing on stucco truss-

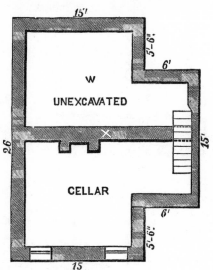

Fig. 36.—PLAN OF CELLAR.

es. It communicates with the living-room and hall. The
remaining wall spaces are unbroken, for furniture and
wall ornaments. The Living-room is a little larger than
the parlor, has two windows, an open fireplace, a closet,
and doors leading to the front hall, parlor, and rear entry. The rear entry is under the platform of the main
stairs ; is divided from the front hall, and is to be used
as the common entrance. It has doors leading from the
front hall, living-room, rear porch, and the cellar stairs.
The parlor may be warmed by placing a radiator under

the marble shelf, and passing the smoke-pipe from the living-room through it, as for Design III. The cost of such a radiator is $6.... SECOND STORY, (fig. 38.)—Hight of center ceilings, seven feet ; hight of side-breast walls, $3^{1}/_{2}$ feet. The stairs leading to this story are made with a platform, placed three risers below the upper landing, which allows for the required head-room. The divisions provide for four rooms, a hall, and two closets ; the large

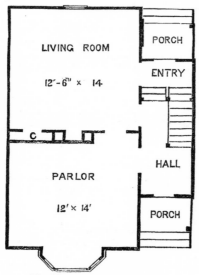

Fig. 37.—PLAN OF FIRST FLOOR.

chamber has a double window in front, a marble shelf on the chimney-breast, and a closet ; the hall bedroom is designed to be used in connection with the large chamber as a child's room.... CONSTRUCTION.—The excavation for the cellar is made four feet deep, and for the rear foundation walls one foot. The loose earth is graded around the foundation at completion, leaving $1^{1}/_{2}$

feet of the foundation exposed to sight on the outside. The foundation walls are of broken stone, laid in common mortar, 16 inches thick, and neatly pointed where exposed to sight, and are generally even with the framework on the outside. Provision is made for the cellar stairway by extending the adjoining walls beyond the inside of the frame to the hight of the ground, and finishing above with brick-work. The chimney is started with the cellar walls, and arranged with two continuous flues

to the top. Side-openings are made under the cap by
inserting 6-inch earthen thimbles on each side of the
flues. The top courses of brick-work are laid across the
entire chimney, making a solid and more lasting cap.
Sheet-iron thimbles are put in the chimneys adjoining
the parlor and front chamber. The framing, inclosing,
flooring, etc., are done in a substantial manner, of materials indicated in the
estimate below.
Beams placed two
feet apart from cen-
ters; rafters and
studding 16 inches
apart. The cornice-
trusses are made of
2×4-inch timber, as
shown in Design VI.,
and the shingling
and gutters in De-
sign V. Sash, 1¹/₄
inch thick, glazed
with second quality
of French sheet-
glass, counter-
checked, and hung

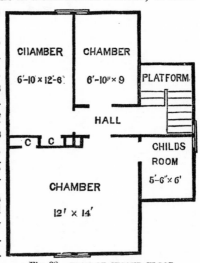

Fig. 38.—PLAN OF SECOND FLOOR.

to iron balance-weights, with good cord. Doors 4-pan-
eled each, for the outside and rooms in first story, and
1¹/₂ inches thick; all others 1¹/₄ inches thick, moulded,
with double faces. The main stairs has a 7-inch octagon
newel, a 2¹/₄×4-inch moulded rail, and 2-inch turned
balusters, all of black walnut. The side-walls and ceilings of the two full stories are white-sand finished, on
one coat of "laid-off" brown mortar. This is the
favorite mode of plastering through the Eastern States,
while in the neighborhood of New York two coats of
brown mortar are usually applied. Where one-coat work

is properly done, more hair is mixed in the mortar, increasing its strength. The *same quantity* of mortar is used as for two coats. The advantages claimed for the "one-coat work" are, a saving of one-third in labor, and obviating the delay for the additional coat to dry. All the wood-work usually painted, and the chimney-top, have two coats of best American lead and *raw* linseed-oil. For more extended remarks on painting, see article with Design XII.

ESTIMATE of materials required, and total cost.

58 yards excavation, at 20c. per yard	$11.60
26 perches stone-work, complete, at $2.50	65.00
2,000 bricks, furnished and laid, complete, at $12 per M	24.00
360 yards plastering, complete, at 25c.	90.00
1,694 ft. timber, at $15 per M	25.41

1 sill, 4×7 in. 26 ft. long.	3 ties, 4×6 in. 15 ft. long.
3 sills, 4×7 in. 15 ft. long.	1 plate, 4×6 in. 26 ft. long.
1 sill, 4×7 in. 23 ft. long.	1 plate, 4×6 in. 23 ft. long.
8 posts, 4×7 in. 13 ft. long.	14 beams, 3×7 in.. 21 ft. long.
1 girt, 4×6 in. 15 ft. long.	13 beams, 3×7 in. 15 ft. long.

20 ceiling-strips, 1¼×5 in. 13 ft. long.

50 joists, 3×4 in. 13 ft. long. at 16c. each	8.00
200 wall-strips, 2×4 in. 13 ft. long, at 13c. each	26.00
130 siding-boards, at 23c. each	29.90
160 shingling-lath, at 6c. each	9.60
40 bunches shingles at $1.25	50.00
12 spruce plank, at 20c.	2.40
Materials in cornices, $14 ; stoops, complete, $20	34.00
95 flooring, at 18c. each	17.10
2 cellar windows, complete, at $3 each	6.00
2 single windows, complete, at $12 each	24.00
3 double windows, complete, at $15 each	45.00
15 doors, complete, at $9 each	135.00
Closet, shelving, and nails	20.00
Stairs, $50 ; bay-window, complete, $50	100.00
Tin (gutters, valleys, and leaders)	11.00
2 marble shelves. $10 ; painting, $80 ; carting, $15	105.00
Carpenter's labor, not included above	100.00
Incidentals, sink, pump, etc.	60.99
Total cost	$1,000.00

DESIGN X.

A HOUSE COSTING $1,100.

This economical cottage has ample, convenient apartments for a medium-sized family, and is adapted to either a village or a more rural location. A 25×100-feet lot will contain such a house, besides the needed side alleyway to the rear. Those contemplating the erection of low-priced, tasteful cottages in duplication, either for selling, or by coöperation as in Building Associations,

Fig. 39.—ELEVATION OF FRONT OF HOUSE.

will find this plan suited to their wants.... EXTERIOR, (fig. 39).—The front presents a graceful, trim, outline, with a neat and pleasant arrangement of openings. The

Porch fits in an angle, with its steps projecting beyond the principal building, providing an appropriate entrance to the house. The large Bay-window is the most impos-ing feature of the front, is expressive of comfort and cheerfulness, and gives a good appearance and character to the whole building. The principal cornices are neatly trussed, and have such "spread" as gives a finished and bold appearance to the roofs. It has such proportions and genteel style, that if near a more formidable or costly residence, it would not disgrace it. . . . . . CELLAR, (figure. 40.)—Hight 7 ft. Its

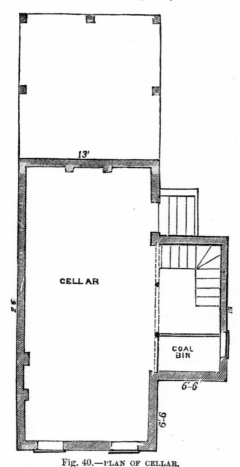

Fig. 40.—PLAN OF CELLAR.

outlines correspond with the ground-plans of the principal building ; it is three feet below the general surface of the ground, and four feet above, and has an outside entrance door, three good sized cellar windows, two of which are in the front, and one at the side, contiguous to the coal-bin. It is accessible from the first story by a plain stairway. If desirable at any time, a pleasant basement room may be finished in the front part, at a small cost..... FIRST STORY, (fig. 41).—Hight of ceilings, $9^1/_2$ feet. It is divided into three rooms of nearly equal size, with a Hall and two Closets. The Bay-window adds considerable to its area, making it the largest and pleasantest

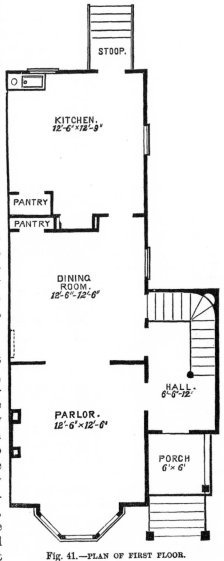

Fig. 41.—PLAN OF FIRST FLOOR.

room. The Dining-room adjoins the parlor, and may be used with it as occasion requires by opening the folding doors. Each of these rooms has neat marble mantles, and opens into the front hall. The Kitchen connects with the dining-room, and is provided with a pantry, pump, sink, two windows, and an outside door leading

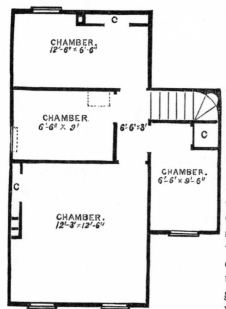

to the rear yard.
When houses are built on single village lots, it is usual to arrange for one " blank " side, as in this plan, but where more ground is allowed, it is desirable that openings should be made for at least one window in each story of this side, as they would add to the cheerfulness of the interior, and give a better appearance to the outside. Two

Fig. 42.—PLAN OF SECOND FLOOR.

windows are thus indicated by dotted lines, one for the dining-room, and one for the interior chamber, though the latter is lighted from the roof, as noted. It may be advisable even to put two other windows on this side of the house, for the outside general good appearance, or blind-windows may be put in at small expense, for the same purpose. . . . SECOND STORY, (fig. 42).—Ceilings 8 feet high. The divisions are very simple, making four rooms, three closets, a stairway, and passage leading to each room.... CONSTRUCTION.—Reference is had in this plan to what is known in the trade as "piece-lumber"— the joists, wall-strips, boards, etc., being generally in lengths of 13 feet each. There is great economy in being able to use such standard lumber, without cutting to waste. Figure 43 shows how a neat, cosey cottage-frame may be cheaply constructed almost wholly of such 13-feet materials. But there is a decided preference for full chamber ceilings, and as the difference in cost would not exceed $60, it is best to make the house *two full stories high*. The principal frame is of 3-inch timber, with studding of 2×3 inch. This thickness of the frame-work se-

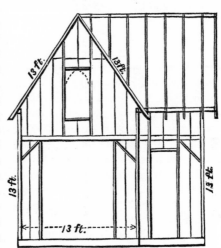

Fig. 43.—MANNER OF FRAMING.

cures some 220 feet more interior space to the rooms, than in the use of 4-inch timber, besides saving one-fourth of its quantity and cost. Ordinary $1^1/_4$×10-inch spruce plank are used for the frame-work, for the floors and ceilings. For the beams they are reduced to the depth of eight inches, and the 2-inch strips sawed off are used for shingling-lath. For the ceiling-frame of the second story, they are simply sawed through the middle, leaving each half five inches deep, and are all placed 16 inches apart from centers. One row of cross-bridging is put through the center of each tier of beams, and the center of the ceiling-strips are secured by hangers from the rafters. The Rafters are 2×4 inches, framed to rest on the principal plates, where they are connected with the ceiling-strips by spikes, preventing any settling or spreading of the roof. The Roof of the main wing is constructed with double pitch, corresponding with that of the main roof. The principal roofs are finished with shingles, and has improved gutters, described in Design V. The porch and bay-window roofs are covered with tin laid on smooth boarding.—The *rake* or *pitch* of roofs has much to do in giving character and finish to buildings. For ordinary roofs, when shingles or slate are used, the rise should be *one-third* the width of the building, as in this case, the rise is $4^1/_3$ feet, for the width of 13 feet. This pitch is very pleasant to the eye, and easy of construction. In larger buildings, it is often desirable to secure more space or head-room in the attic, when the rise should be *one-half* the width of the building. We would never go *between* these two angles in search of a roof-line that would gratify good taste, or comport with any style, but deviations above one-half or below one-third may be made, as circumstances indicate.—Circular openings covered with blinds, in each gable, give free air circulation between the ceilings and roof. Every dwelling should have some way of readily reaching the roof from the inside to clean the gutters, repair the roof or chimneys, and in case of fire in the house or in the neighborhood. An opening is made in the ceiling of the middle chamber (fig. 42) over and just inside the door, and thence through the roof. This is neatly boarded around its sides, forming a "well," and is covered at the top with a *sash*, sloping with the roof, hung so as to be easily opened and closed by a cord from the inside. This provides for light, ventilation, and a scuttle in combination. A sash, hung on center pins to revolve, over the door of this room, transmits light from the sky-light to the second-story passage and stairway, and supplies ventilation.... The mason's work is complete and substantial in every part. The foundation walls, piers, and chimneys, are of hard brick and mortar; the plastering is two coats of brown mortar and a hard finish.... HEATING.—Only two fires are required at any time to make the principal rooms of this house comfortable. The parlor, and chamber immediately above it, are warmed through a heater placed in a parlor fire-place. The dining-room has a radiator fitted in the opening of the mantel, and connected by 5-inch pipes through the fire-place back with the kitchen stove.

ESTIMATE of materials and cost:

40 yards excavation, at 20c. per yard	$ 8.00
12,000 brick. furnished and laid, at $12 per M	144.00
32 ft. stone steps and coping, at 20c. per ft	6.40
450 yards plastering. at 30c. per yard	135.00
1,969 ft. of timber, at $15 per M	29.53

1 sill, 4×8 in. 39 ft. long.	6 posts, 3×8 in. 20 ft. long.
1 girt, 4×8 in. 13 ft. long.	1 tie, 3×6 in. 104 ft. long.
1 plate, 3×4 in. 104 ft. long.	1 sill. 2×4 in. 91 ft. long.
116 studding. 2×3 in. 10 ft. long.	153 studding, 2×3 in. 9 ft. long.

70 planks for beams and ceilings, at 25c. each	17.50
55 rafters, 2×4×13, at 13c. each	7.15
208 siding, 10 inch, at 26c. each	54.08
100 lbs. tarred felting, at 3c. per lb.	3.00
Materials in cornices, water-table, and corner-boards	20.00
165 shingling-lath, at 6c. each	9.90
28 bunches shingles, at $1.50 per bunch	42.00
200 ft. gutters. leaders and roofs, at 8c. per ft	16.00
96 flooring, at 26c. each	24.96
Stairs, complete, $40 ; porch and stoops, complete, $40	80.00
Bay-window, complete	60 00
8 windows, complete, at $10 each	80.00
3 cellar windows, complete, at $6 each	18.00
15 doors, complete, at $8 each	120.00
Closets and shelving. $8: mantels, $30	38.00
Pump and sink, $18; nails, $15	33.00
Painting, $60 : cartage, $13.48	73.48
Carpenter's labor, not included above	80.00
Total cost, complete	$1,100.00

DESIGN XI.

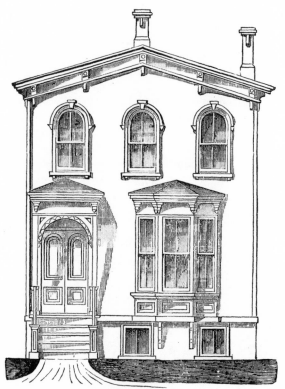

Fig. 44.—FRONT ELEVATION OF HOUSE.

A HOUSE COSTING $1,600.

This plan is for a comfortable and genteel dwelling, suited to almost any location, and for the accommodation of an averaged-sized family. Upwards of twenty years' experience in planning and building has taught me that it is not difficult to design either as to Style, Room, or Cost, when the owners have means sufficient to gratify their individual tastes, and no special care is required to save expense. But it is quite another matter to provide plans for the great mass of people who, through habit or necessity, put everything to the test of economy, and to whom every inch of room, or foot of material, is an important consideration. In designing and projecting such work, theories avail little ; practical experience must then be the chief guide... Conventional modes of living have established a system of household ar-

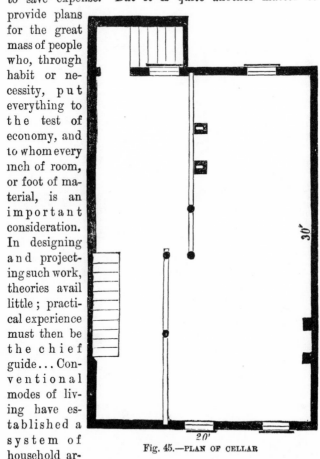

Fig. 45.—PLAN OF CELLAR

rangement and economy requiring for every home of even moderate refinement, a house with a front hall, a parlor, a dining-room, and a kitchen on the first floor,

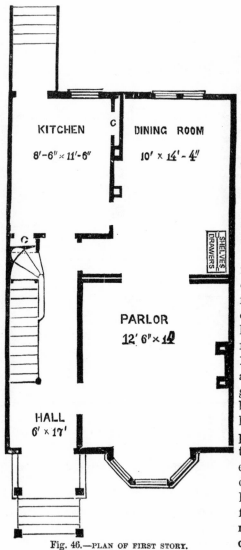

KITCHEN

8'-6" × 11'-6"

DINING ROOM

10' × 14'-4"

SHELVES
DRAWERS

PARLOR

12' 6" × 14

HALL

6' × 17'

Fig. 46.—PLAN OF FIRST STORY.

and a liberal suite of chambers in a second story. Our plan herewith, though only 20 by 30 feet, provides for all the above. If built on an ordinary 25-feet village lot, it will allow a needed passage - way on one side. In rapidly filling up, crowded localities, four persons owning single lots, making a frontage of 100 feet, can arrange together and build five houses on this plan for about the cost of erecting four detached houses. The fifth house may be rented or sold for the benefit of the four owners. In such cases, a hall should be finished in the basement, with an entrance in front similar to the one shown in the rear in fig. 45.... The FRONT ELEVATION is made up of simple parts, in a neat arrangement. The Bay-window indicates refinement, and adds largely to the area or room of the parlor. .... The CELLAR walls are of hard brick, are 8 inches thick, 7 feet high, and show at least 3 feet above ground. For health's sake alone, as well as for a better appearance, and for convenience, if the basement should ever be desired fin-

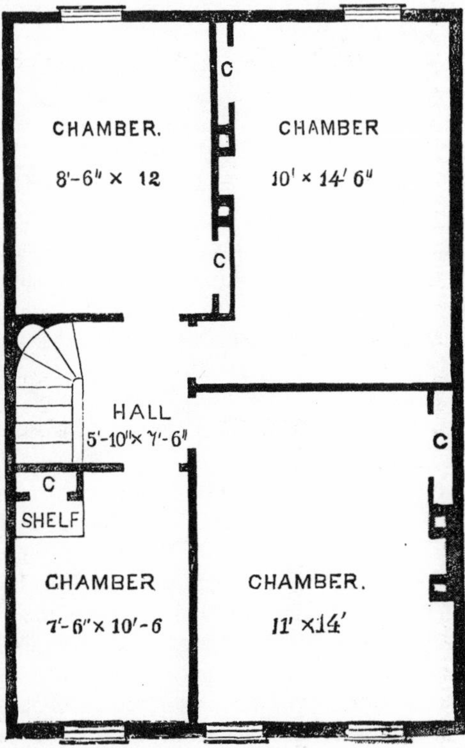

Fig. 47.—PLAN OF SECOND STORY.

ished off in rooms, which can be done at any time with little expense, it is best to always place the first floor well up from the ground. In very cold localities, frost can be kept out of the basement by banking up in winter, or better by laying the brick walls with an opening up through the center, extending bricks across the opening at frequent intervals to secure firmness. This central air-chamber promotes health, warmth, and dryness in the basement or cellar. One foot of the soil taken from the excavation for the cellar should be used in grading around the house, to secure the flow of water *away* from it, and still leave the walls three feet or more above the ground.... FIRST STORY, (fig. 46).—Hight of ceiling, $9^{1}/_{2}$ feet. The divisions embrace three rooms, a hall, and two closets. Double doors are provided for the front entrance, and between the parlor and dining-room, and marble mantles and shelves in the principal rooms. A movable "Dresser" having drawers and shelving with small doors, is indicated for the dining-room. This room may be heated by leading a pipe from the kitchen stove to a drum and back into the chimney, or up through the chamber above to warm that somewhat. A "Fireplace heater" in the parlor will warm the chamber above.... SECOND STORY, (fig. 47.)—The hight of the ceilings are $8^{1}/_{2}$ feet. There are four chambers, with closets to each, and a small hall. The head-room over the main stairs extends beneath the closet to the inner edge of the shelf shown—the floor in these parts being angled to suit the pitch of the stairs.... REMARKS on construction.—An end section of the "Novelty siding" is shown in fig. 48. This is of 10-inch boards, 1 inch thick, cut as shown in the engraving. The groove in the center gives it the appearance of narrow clapboards ; the lap of about an inch closes tightly, and the thick boards not only add to the warmth, but also to the strength. A house covered with this will vibrate very little in the most windy situations, and be firmer than one covered with thin siding having much heavier timber. Where planing mills are accessible, it is little more expensive than the dressed half-inch boarding, and the appearance is quite as pretty. In this vicinity it is customary to

Fig. 48.—"NOVELTY SIDING."

purchase a lot of pretty good quality merchantable pine boards, select the best and clearest of knots for siding, and use the rest for flooring where knots are not objectionable when to be covered with carpeting. The smaller and firm knots in the siding used, are readily covered with paint, if first primed with a little solution of shellac in alcohol. A section of the wall is shown in fig. 49. The studding, 2×4, makes a space of four inches between the siding and plastering. Tarred paper, or what is termed roofing-felt, is procured in rolls 32 inches wide. A saw run through the roll cuts it into 16-inch strips. The studs being set 16 inches apart from center to center, leaves the clear space of 14 inches. The strips of felt are turned up an inch on each

Fig. 49.—SECTION OF OUTSIDE WALL.

edge, and these turned edges are held against the studs by lath firmly up and down, so as to hold the sheets midway between the plastering and siding. This leaves *two* air-chambers, both good non-conductors of heat. Mice or insects will not eat or go through this material. It is impervious to currents of air, and the whole is as warm as if filled in with brick. The cost is very small, and, as will be readily seen, it is much warmer than when the felt is put on directly under the boards, leaving only one air-chamber, and that a wide one.... In all house-plans, we advise putting in all the closets possible ; they are always convenient, even a foot square " cubby-hole " in the side of a chimney is a handy place. In planning a house, after making the size as large as one's means will allow, the "better half" should be consulted as to the advisability of making this or that room a little smaller by cutting off a few inches here and there to enlarge a pantry or closet.... We always advise to put in an extra bell or two, and one or more speaking-tubes, to connect the upper and lower rooms. The cost is but trifling, if they are put in when building. A hundred feet of speaking-tube will cost but $2 or $3 ; the carpenter can insert it behind the lath, running it from one room to another in a few minutes, and it will save many steps, and much calling through the halls, especially when the mother happens to be an invalid, and restrained to a chamber . . . In arranging sink, table, dish-pantry, etc., with reference to dining-room and kitchen, always plan to save steps. A distance of 10 feet extra, traveled over each way, say 20 times a day, in handling food and dishes, amounts to 28 miles extra walking every year, all of which may be saved by a slight change in arrangement. These are small matters, but these have much to do in making a " convenient house."

Cost.—The following Estimates of cost in detail will give an idea of the general character of the work. The prices given are for materials in the vicinity of New York. Carpenters wages are reckoned at $2 per day ; mason's work, $2.50 per day ; and painters, $3 per day :

Excavation, 2½ ft. deep, at 20c. per yard	$11.00
12,000 hard brick, furnished and laid, at $12 per M	144.00
28 ft. stone steps, at 40c. per ft	11.20
16 ft. stone sills, at 30c. per ft	4.80
483 yards lath and plastering, at 30c	144.90
2,000 ft. timber, at $15 per M	30.00

2 sills, 4×7 in. 20 ft. long.	2 ties, 4×6 in. 26 ft. long.
2 sills, 4×7 in. 30 ft. long.	2 ties, 4×6 in. 30 ft. long.
4 posts, 4×7 in. 20 ft. long.	2 girders, 4×8 in. 15 ft. long.
2 plates, 4×6 in. 20 ft. long.	2 stringers, 3×8 in. 20 ft. long.
2 plates, 4×6 in. 30 ft. long.	30 beams, 3×8 in. 20 ft. long.

32 rafters, 3×4 in. 12 feet long, at 18c	5 76
300 wall-strips. 2×4 in. 13 ft. long. at 11c	33.00
200 novelty siding-boards, 9½ in., at 30c	60.00
160 lbs. tarred paper, at 5c	8.00
100 hemlock boards, 10 in., at 18c	18.00
100 ft. main cornice, at 40c	40 00
1 bay-window, complete, with blinds, labor included	60.00
1½ stoops, complete. labor included	70.00
8 windows with blinds, at $16	128.00
4 windows with blinds, at $8	32.00
8½ squares of tin roofing, at $7	59.50
100 ft. gutters and leaders. at 10c	10.00
150 flooring-plank, tongued and grooved, at 28c	42.00
Stairs, main and cellar, $60 ; base-boards, shelving, etc.. $30	90.00
4 mantels (1 full marble, and 3 marble shelves on trusses of plaster).	50.00
21 doors, complete, labor included, $158; 350 lbs. nails, at 5c., $17.50..	175.50
Painting, two coats	80.00
Carpenter's labor, not included in windows, doors, and porches, about $200.00; cartage, average one mile, $30 00	230.00
Allow for extras, cistern, pump, sink, etc., etc	62.34
Total	$1,600.00

Prices vary in different localities, somewhat, but when higher in some particulars, they will generally be lower in others, so that the whole cost will not be greatly different over a considerable extent of country. There are many items that can be cut down in the above estimate, where great economy is needful. For example, substitute wood for stone steps and sills ; omit the blinds and bay-windows, use cheaper doors, pine-stair railing and newel, instead of walnut, etc. Our estimate is for a pretty, complete, tasteful house.

DESIGN XII.

A HOUSE COSTING $1,700.

The plans here given are similar in many respects to Design XI., and are somewhat larger, but can be built for very nearly the same cost.... ELEVATION, (fig. 50).— The front is irregular, having an angle, which narrows the parts, supplies more vertical lines, and adds to their length comparatively. These are important features, imparting a graceful appearance, and influencing the entire character of the house..... The angle affords ample room for the piazza, which can be built for much less cost than when its three sides are exposed. The next attractive features of the front are the bay-windows below, and double windows above, with the balustrade and hood so proportioned and arranged that they conform with each other with pleasing effect..... CELLAR, (fig. 51).—The Foundation Walls are of hard brick laid in mortar, 8 inches thick, and 7 feet high. In localities where the foundation rests on loose sand, care should be taken to provide a bedding, laid 4 inches below the cellar bottom, 16 inches wide, of brick, or better, of large flat stones. Still greater care should be bestowed on the

Fig. 50.—ELEVATION OF FRONT.

bedding for the chimneys and girder supports, for they sustain the greatest proportionate weight, and any settlement of these parts will cause a depression of the floors, disarranging the whole house, and become an immediate and continuous source of anxiety and expense. The Area in the rear is built of hard brick and mortar, with blue-stone steps and coping. Blue-stone sills are provided for each of the cellar windows.... FIRST STORY, (fig. 52.)—

The interior arrangement of the plan will be appreciated as making the best possible use of the room. The Front Hall is wider than is usual in houses of this character. The Stairs are arranged with the "quarter circle" about midway of their hight, which brings the niche down where it becomes an important feature of the hall. The three principal rooms, the parlor, dining-

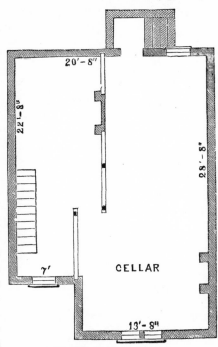

Fig. 51.—PLAN OF CELLAR.

room, and kitchen, can be entered from the hall. The latter two rooms have doors leading to the lobby. The Lobby is built of 4½-inch tongued and grooved ceiling-boards, with sashes made to swing. A Shelf, 1½ feet high, and another just above the sash, give sufficient frame-work to fasten the center of the boarding; the ends are nailed to the sill and plate; these shelves will be found useful for many purposes. Attached to the lobby, and built with it, is a good-sized Pantry (*P*), for the dining-room. The Kitchen is provided with a closet at the side of the chimney, a sink, with small closet un-

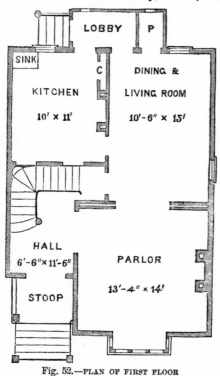

derneath, and a direct communication to the cellar stairs under the hall stairs. The window in the side of the dining-room may be omitted, if the house is in a village and joins another, but this is desirable to give abundant light in this, which is really the living-room of the family.— The method of heating indicated in Design XI. are applicable to this plan... SECOND STORY, (fig 52.)—The pecu-

Fig. 52.—PLAN OF FIRST FLOOR

liar manner of constructing the Stairs brings their landing nearly in the center, so that hall space sufficient only for four doors is necessary, leaving almost the entire floor to be laid off into rooms. The heavy lines show the most simple method of dividing this story into four rooms. Should another room be desirable, it can be taken off from two rooms, as shown by the dotted lines. In this case, another window may be inserted as indicated. Every one's experience will suggest that there can not be too many closets, and we have added one to every room in the house, except the parlor.... CONSTRUCTION.— The bill of timber appended indicates a "regular" *Frame.* It is a great satisfaction and saving to have the timber properly "laid out," and framed by, and under the immediate direction of a master mechanic, so as to be quickly and substantially raised. Four good carpenters would easily frame all the timber in this house in two days, and raise it the next day. At least one man of well-known ability and experience as a mechanic should be with

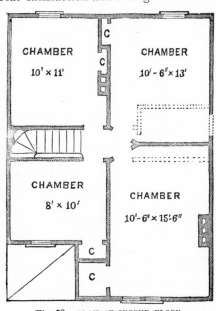

Fig. 53.—PLAN OF SECOND FLOOR.

and take charge of those employed to build a house. It is not economical for one about to build a *home* to trust such work to the caprice of an inexperienced man, who has "helped" around some job, until he has learned the name of tools, but who has no positive knowledge of the trade, and could not for his life "lay out" the corner-post for a two-story house, yet is shrewd enough to screen his deficiencies by suggesting "balloon," or something indefinite, that requires little or no skill. It sometimes

happens, in localities remote from large cities or large
towns, that persons are obliged to do with make-shifts, to
get a home at all. It was such a condition of things that led
the well-disposed pioneer of the West to adopt the method
called "Balloon framing," which is really no framing at
all, and required no skill to get up a kind of home ac-
ceptable under such circumstances. But wherever skilled
labor may be had, it is ridiculous to see a gang of intelligent (?) mechanics standing up pieces of diverse lengths,
and propping them in a vertical position with rods running every way as braces, not one of which can be removed until the upper ends are secured by ties of some
sort. A good frame in a house is equivalent to a good
constitution in a man, and is of vital importance ; it need
not be clumsy or overloaded, but should at least have the
merit of being able to stand alone.... PAINTING.—The
principal object in Painting should be to protect and
preserve the materials used in construction, as also to
give a good appearance. All exterior wood-work, though
executed with the greatest care and in the most substantial manner, if left exposed to climatic influences, is very
soon destroyed. It is economy to use only the *best lead*
and *linseed-oil* in painting exterior wood-work. They
will outlast all other compounds, present a better appearance, and in the end furnish a much better foundation
for future painting. The difference in cost between the
best materials and the imitations, for painting the exterior of a house built on these plans, would not exceed
$12, and the cost of labor would be just the same in
either case. The first coat or "priming," should be put
on with the greatest care, so as to thoroughly cover and
close all the pores in the exposed surface. All window
and outside door frames, corner-boards, window-caps,
water-table, and stoop-flooring, should be primed *before*
setting, especially their edges, where joinings require to
be made, as it will be the last opportunity to do justice

to these parts, where moisture is liable to collect and remain. When priming is well done, it is best to let the building stand until thoroughly dried, both inside and out, before adding the second coat. It must be evident to any one that much of the water used in the plastering must percolate through, and thoroughly saturate every part of a house. Sufficient time should be allowed for this moisture to pass off, and the whole house to become dried out.... The nails should then be "set," which will tighten up permanently all the laps in the siding, after which the work should be properly puttied, and the second coat applied. Autumn is the best season to paint, after the extreme heat has passed, and insects have disappeared; the process of drying will be slower and more perfect, with less waste by evaporation, leaving a smooth, solid surface. I am often asked *"what color to paint?"* Notwithstanding much has been said against white for outside painting, and realizing that there are many cases where white would not be suitable, or thought of, yet I believe that for suitability and good taste, in nine cases out of ten, very light colors, or pure white, are indicated. I have known instances where much time has been spent to discover a suitable color for a house, where nearly all the different pigments were drawn from, and after much mixing and testing, the result has generally been an unknown and unnamed shade, as if everything depended on some sentimental "blending with the background," or in other words, painting the house out of sight. As a rule, paint so as to best reveal the true character of the building, and this is best done when the colors afford the foundation for the natural shadows that result from the true and actual projections. For the body and trimmings are suggested a light "Dorchester" gray; roofs, graphite-black; sash, coach-black; blinds, "chocolate."

COST.—The following items, prepared with care, embrace the full bill of materials and labor required in the construction of this house, together with their present cost in the vicinity of New York :

57 yards excavation, at 20c. per yard	$11.40
13,000 brick, furnished and laid, at $12 per M	156.00
500 yards lath and plastering, at 30c. per yard	150.00
28 ft. stone steps and coping, at 40c. per ft	11.20
16 ft. stone sills, at 30c. per ft	4.80
2,370 feet of timber, at $15 per M	35.55

2 sills, 4×7 in. 30 ft. long.	6 posts, 4×7 in. 20 ft. long.
2 sills, 4×7 in. 22 ft. long.	2 ties, 4×6 in. 30 ft. long.
1 girt, 4×8 in. 16 ft. long.	2 ties, 4×6 in. 22 ft. long.
1 girt, 4×8 in. 8 ft. long.	2 plates, 4×6 in. 30 ft. long.
26 beams, 3×7 in. 22 ft. long.	2 plates, 4×6 in. 22 ft. long.
6 beams, 3×7 in. 15 ft. long.	4 pieces, 3×7 in. 16 ft. long.

400 wall-strips, 2×4 in. 13 ft. long, at 11c. each	44.00
200 novelty siding-boards, 1¼ in., at 30c. each	60.00
160 lbs. tarred paper, at 5c. per lb	8.00
128 tongued and grooved flooring, 9¼ in., at 35c. each	44.80
110 hemlock boards, at 18c. each	19.80
9½ squares of tin roofing, at $7 per square	66.50
120 ft. cornice, at 30c. per ft	36.00
111 ft. gutter and leader, at 10c. per ft	11.10
1 bay-window, with blinds, complete	60.00
Materials in stoop, lobby, balcony, hood, and corner-boards	78.00
8 windows, with blinds, complete, at $16 each	128.00
4 cellar windows, complete, at $4 each	16.00
24 doors, complete, at $8 each	192.00
2 stairs, complete	60.00
2 marble mantels and 4 pine mantels	75.00
Base-boards and shelving	25.00
Nails, sink, and pump	34.00
Cartage, average one mile	30.00
Carpenter's labor (not included above)	200.00
Painting, two coats	80.00
Extra for girder supports, grading, etc	62.85
Total cost of materials and construction	**$1,700.00**

DESIGN XIII.

FRENCH-ROOFED COTTAGE, COSTING $2,000.

These plans were designed for a genteel cottage adapted to thickly-settled localities, where the increased value of lands make it necessary to reduce the area, and build upwards. Several houses constructed from these plans in this vicinity are admired for their convenient accommodation and cheerfulness..... EXTERIOR, (fig. 54.)—The Foundation extends four feet above ground, giving a desirable altitude to the whole building. The front is enlivened by the numerous window and door openings, the several projections of piazza, dormers, and cornices, and the variety of the materials used. The dressing of the several parts are of simple designs. The projections of cornices, etc., should always be self-sustaining, yet while this is true, there is sure to be a fancied necessity for some apparent support obvious from the out-side. Such supports require special treatment, with a view to their proper form and proportion, and should be spar-ingly applied, giving to each one its distinct place and pur-pose. Brackets of neat pattern are often crowd-ed so closely to-gether as to cheapen and de-stroy their beauty, and overload the cor-nice, thus re-

Fig. 54.—ELEVATION OF FRONT OF HOUSE.

versing their legitimate purpose as supports.... CELLAR, fig. 55.)—Hight of ceiling 7 feet; it extends under the main house only. Its hight above the ground gives an opportunity for good-sized window openings. If desired at any time, an airy and light work-room or laundry can be made by dividing and flooring a part of this story at

little cost.... First Story, (fig. 56).—Hight of ceiling
10 feet. It has a hall running through the whole length
of the main house, with entrances from both front and

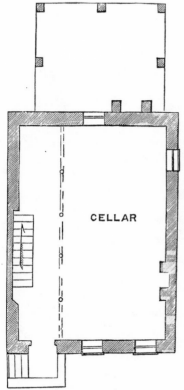

rear. The parlor, din-
ing-room, and kitchen,
are all good-sized apart-
ments, and pleasantly
arranged. Double fold-
ing doors are provided
for the front entrances
and from the hall to
the parlor, and sliding
doors between the par-
lor and dining - room.
A bay-window adds ma-
terially to the size and
pleasantness of the din-
ing or living-room.
Each room has an open
fire-place; the kitchen
has a pump and sink,
with the usual supply
and waste-pipe connec-
tions. The rear stoop
is roofed, and has a
portable enclosure of
light ceiling boards, to
be used in severe weath-
er.... Second Story,

Fig. 55.—PLAN OF CELLAR.   (fig. 57.) — Hight of

ceiling $8\frac{1}{2}$ feet. The divisions of this story are simple—
giving a hall, two large chambers, with passage between,
two hall rooms, and two closets.... Construction.—The
estimate given provides for foundation of broken stone,
laid and neatly pointed with good mortar; the stone exposed to sight on the outside to be "semi-dressed."

Blue-stone, or other suitable stone obtained most readily, are used for the sills of cellar windows, for the steps, and wall coping of the cellar entrance. The principal timber is of seasoned spruce or pine, thoroughly framed, raised, and secured. The " framing-in " of braces is too frequently omitted— cutting them " barefoot," and spiking, being substituted. The latter does very well where the frame is strongly sheathed over, and the outer siding applied afterwards. The sheathing aids largely in stiffening the frame, but should not be relied on to the exclusion of the necessary braces to square up the frame, and pre-

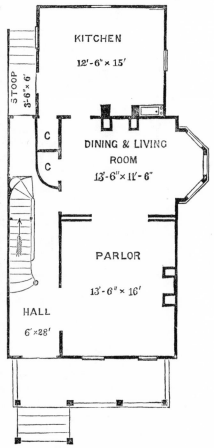

Fig. 56.—PLAN OF FIRST FLOOR.

vent the swaying which often happens unobserved, to be discovered when too late to remedy it. Laxity in the matter of bracing has led to frequent errors as to their proper place in the frame. When framed in they are invariably placed in the *upper angles* under the ties and plates, adjoining the posts, and when barefoot they should be put in the same angles; never, as is frequently done for convenience, in the lower angles, nor on the sills. A moment's reflection will convince any one that

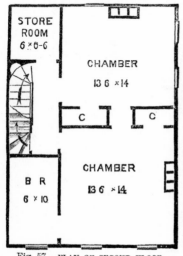

CHAMBER

13 6 × 14

C   C

CHAMBER

B R   13 6 × 14

6 × 10

Fig. 57.—PLAN OF SECOND FLOOR.

if the right angles along the principal frame are rigidly maintained, displacements will never occur, except, as rarely happens, the whole is bodily raised from the foundation by a hurricane. The most *reliable* angles are those formed by the tie and post connections, b e c a u s e at these points the posts are tenoned and mortised together, and secured with hard wood pins. Those least reliable are at the foot of the posts, adjoining the sills, where their connections are secured only by the weight of the upper frame. Braces placed in the latter angles serve only as fulcrums to endanger the frames when tested by ordinary winds ; but if the former or *upper* angles are made positive, by having substantial braces in them, the severest gales may be defied. The siding is of narrow, clear pine clapboards, laid on "thicknessed" sheathing. The Mansard part of the main roof is covered by 8×16-inch slate—the piazza, bay-window, kitchen, stoop, cornices, window, and deck roof with I. C. charcoal tin—all laid on hemlock boards. Tarred felting is spread under all siding and slate. The first and second stories are fully completed inside ; the attic is floored, but otherwise unfinished, but may be divided at any time into rooms as shown for the second story (fig. 57). The interior plastering is three-coat work, on seasoned lath. All sash are four lights, and hung to balance-weights. Blinds are properly hung (outside) to each window. All wood, tin, and brick-work, usually painted, has two coats of best lead and oil-paint, with stainers to suit the owner's taste. The choice of colors for the exterior is frequently canvassed during the construction of these buildings ; often some person of *taste* (?) decides by " warming "—adding red and yellow, until, by the preponderance of these stainers, the most sombre and dismal colors are produced. The most appropriate and pleasing shade for the body of this class of house is a *light gray ;* for the trimmings, *dark gray ;* for the sash, *burnt sienna ;* for the blinds, *chocolate.* The tin roofing should match the *slate* in color. Red colors should be sparingly used, or omitted altogether.

ESTIMATE of materials required, and total cost :

50 yards excavation. at 25c. per yard	$12.50
975 ft. of stone foundation, at 8c. per ft	78.00
45 ft. blue-stone sills, steps. and coping, at 30c. per ft	13.50
4,000 bricks, furnished and laid, at $12 per M	48.00
480 yards plastering, at 30c. per yard	144.00
Cornices and centers, stucco	30.00
4.000 ft. of timber, at $15 per M	60.00

2 sills, 4×8 in. 29 ft. l'ng | 6 ties, 4×6 in. 21 ft. long | 2 decks, 3×8 in. 18 ft. long
2 sills, 4×8 in. 21 ft. l'ng | 2 plates, 4×6 in. 13 ft. long | 2 decks, 3×8 in. 26 ft. long
1 sill, 4×8 in. 16 ft. long | 1 plate, 4×6 in. 16 ft. long | 1 cross-tie. 3×8 in. 18 ft. l'ng
2 sills, 4×8 in. 13 ft. l'ng | 2 posts, 4×6 in. 13 ft. long | 4 hips, 3×7 in. 14 ft. long
1 girt. 4×8 in. 29 ft. l'ng | 30 beams,3×8 in. 21 ft. l'ng | 2 piazzas, 3×7 in. 19 ft. long
6 posts, 4×7 in. 22 ft. l'g | 15 beams, 3×7 in. 21 ft. l'ng | 2 piazzas, 3×7 in. 18 ft. long
6 ties, 4×6 in. 29 ft. long | 7 beams. 3×8 in. 16 ft. l'ng

325 wall-strips, at 12c. each, $39; 75 joists, at 16c. each. $12	51.00
210 hemlock boards, at 12c. each. $25.20; cornice materials, $60	85.20
215 sheathing, at 16c. each, $34.40 : 560 pine siding, at 12c. each, $67.20	101.60
8 squares slate, at $8.50 per square	68.00
13 squares tin, at $7.50 per square	97.50
65 ft. leaders, at 10c. per ft.. $6.50; 260 flooring, at 18c. each, $46.80	53.30
Piazza and stoop, complete, $80 and $28	108.00
4 cellar windows, complete, at $4 each	16.00
5 plain windows, complete. at $12 each	60.00
6 plain windows, complete. at $10 each, $60; 1 bay window, $60	120.00
5 dormer windows, complete. at $16 each	80.00
13 doors. complete, at $10 each	130.00
1 area door, $5; stairs, $90 : closets, pump, and sink, $50	145.00
Mantle, $52; tarred felting, $10	62.00
Carpenter's labor, not inclued above	135.00
Carting, average 1 mile, $30 ; painting, $130 ; incidentals, $141.40	301.40
Total cost, complete	**$2,000.00**

DESIGN XIV.

Fig. 58.—ELEVATION OF FRONT OF HOUSE.

A FRENCH-ROOFED COTTAGE COSTING $2,000.

These plans were designed for a cottage recently built by Mr. W. W. Billings, in New London, Conn. These sketches embrace also the outlines of the grounds immediately surrounding. The site faces a street having steep grades, conforming to the general declivity upon which a large part of the city is built. The grounds are raised above the sidewalk, and leveled in front, and are faced with stonework from $2\frac{1}{2}$ feet high at left, to 6 feet high at the right. The rear grounds are 6 feet higher than those in front. The step A, at the entrance (see fig. 59),

is 8 inches above the sidewalk. *B* is the bottom of the
cellar, 2 feet 2 inches higher than *A*, and is solid rock.
The walk leading from *A* to the rear ascends $1^{1}/_{4}$ inch to
the foot ; the banks at either side are terraced, and have
stone steps inserted in them leading to the flagging at
the foot of the
porch steps, and
also to the area,
or cellar en-
trance.... ELE-
VATION, (fig.
58.) — The
French roof
style is well
adapted to this
situation on ac-
count of its
rounded and
solid appear-
ance. The irreg-
ularities of out-
line secure
agreeable fea-
tures of variety

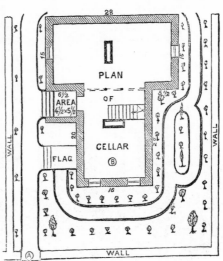

Fig. 59.—PLAN OF CELLAR AND GROUNDS.

and picturesqueness. The Foundation shows 4 feet
above ground in front, and 1 foot in the rear. The
Porch is in an angle, and the second story extending over
it is carried up vertically past the slated part of the main
roof, forming a tower-like corner. This corner is largely
supported by a single column, and to make it as light as
possible, slating of this portion is omitted.—(*As usually
laid, slate weighs* 500 *lbs. ; tin,* 50 *lbs. per square.*)....
CELLAR, (fig. 59.)—Hight is $6^{1}/_{2}$ feet. Four windows
are placed where they give light to every part. An outside door opens to the area, the latter being covered by
the front porch. The front portion of this cellar can

easily be finished off for a work-room or summer kitchen.
.... FIRST STORY, fig. 60.)—Hight of ceiling 10 feet.
The arrangements are convenient, comprising a hall,
parlor, dining-room, and kitchen. The main entrance
leads from the right of the porch, and the hall runs

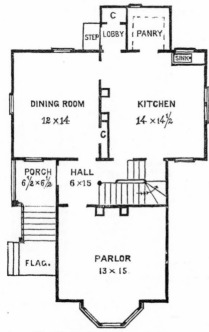

parallel with the
front. Many per-
sons prefer the
entrance ar-
ranged in this
way, as the con-
tents of the hall
are not exposed
to the street
whenever the
doors are opened
or left ajar. A
partition crosses
the hall under the
platform, adjoin-
ing the cylinder,
forming a rear
passage leading
from the kitchen
to the cellar
stairs. The Par-
lor has a large
bay - window in

Fig. 60.—PLAN OF FIRST FLOOR.

front, with a marble mantle directly opposite. The Dining-Room and Kitchen each have windows giving views
in three directions. The small wing at the rear contains
a good-sized pantry, closet, and the rear entrance or
lobby.... SECOND STORY, (fig. 61.)—Hight of ceiling
9 feet. The divisions include a hall, three large chambers, a bedroom, and three closets. All parts are well
lighted. Ventilating Registers are placed in the center

of each chamber ceiling. The space above this ceiling under the tin roof is ventilated through 8-inch pipes inserted in opposite sides of the roof. These pipes have funnel-shaped covers, elevated two inches above the upper end of the pipes.... CONSTRUCTION.—The Foundation

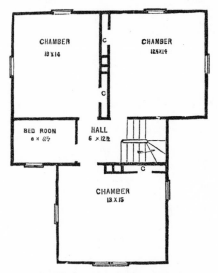

Fig. 61.—PLAN OF SECOND FLOOR.

Walls are of semi-dressed stone. The Chimneys are of hard brick, the cellar portions are constructed with a hollow space or ash-pit, arranged to receive the ashes from the fires of the first story. The siding is beveled clap-boards, laid on sheathing felt. The mansard parts of the main roof are covered with 8×16-inch Keystone slate laid on felt. All other roofs are of IC. charcoal tin, all laid on seasoned boards. The two full stories are hard finished upon two coats of brown mortar. All parts usually painted have two coats of paint, of material and shades to suit the owner. For suggestions on selecting colors or shades see Design XIII.—ESTIMATE cost of materials and labor :

46 yards excavation, at 20c. per yard	$9.20
1,300 ft. stone foundation, at 15c. per ft....	195.00
40 ft. blue-stone, at 25c. per ft.	10.00
5,000 bricks in chimney, at $12 per M	60.00
700 yards plastering, at 30c. per yard	210.00
3,650 ft. timber, at $15 per M	54.75
100 joists, at 14c.. $14 ; 400 wall-strips, at 11c., $44	58.00
1,660 ft. siding, at 2¾c. per ft.	45.65
Cornice materials, $70 ; felt, $10	80.00
220 rough boards, at 15c. each	33.00
9 squares slate, at $9 per square	81.00
13 squares tin, at $7.50	97.50
194 spruce flooring, at 20c. each	38.80
14 pine flooring, at 25c. each	3 50
4 cellar windows, complete, at $3 each	12.00
8 plain windows, complete, at $12 each	96.00
1 bay window, complete	50.00
7 dormer windows, at $14	98.00
Porch, finished, $22 ; mantles, $50	72.00
Stairs, $65 ; nails, sink, and ventilator, $32	97.00
Closet, finished, $13 ; painting, $150	163.00
18 doors, complete, at $9 each	162.00
Carting, $25 ; labor, not included above, $225	250.00
Incidentals	23.60
Total cost, complete	$2,000.00

——————

DESIGN XV.

A SOUTHERN HOUSE COSTING $2,000.

These plans, designed for a Georgia residence, will be adapted to the requirements of others desiring to build an inexpensive rural home in any of the Southern States. .... EXTERIOR, (fig. 62.)—The plan indicates that the proprietor is not circumscribed by want of land, and prefers to extend the area of the ground floor, rather than to build upward. The breadth of the front (48 feet), the large entrance and window openings, the spacious verandas, and broad steps, are each prominent and desirable features, indicative of comforts and hospitality. The elevated, or second story part of the Main House, forms a substantial and fitting center, around which the roofs of the wings and verandas incline, and adds largely in giving poise and character to the whole building. The hight from the earth grades to the frame-work of the building is 2 feet. Its location should have a good

Fig. 62.—FRONT VIEW OF HOUSE.

surface drainage assured during rainy seasons, and afford pleasant outlooks from the verandas.... INTERIOR.—In most parts of the South, very much of the year could be comfortably spent out of doors altogether, but for the requirements of shade and retirement.   There are times,

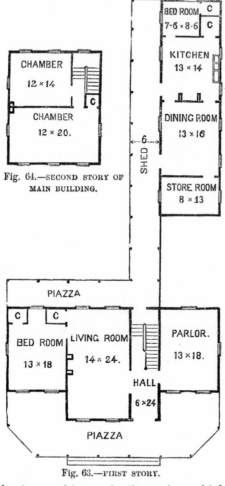

Fig. 64.—SECOND STORY OF MAIN BUILDING.

Fig. 63.—FIRST STORY.

however, when severe weather makes it necessary that one's family should be well housed, and when a good fire is both a luxury and necessity.   A house for such a latitude should have large rooms, with high ceilings, an abundance of door and window openings, and a plentiful spread of shady verandas. Where practicable, the windows should have folding sashes opening to the floor, if protected by outside coverings.   There should be at least one chimney in the main or highest part of the house, having a large open fire-place adapted to the use

of wood for fuel, and having openings near the room ceilings into the flues, for ventilation. The Dining-room,
Kitchen, and the more domestic offices, require a separate and distinct building, situated a short distance in
the rear of the house, and connected with it by a covered
passage-way.... FIRST STORY, (fig. 63.)—Hight of ceiling 10 feet. The simple arrangement shown provides for
each of the above requirements. The front Entrance is
through large double doors. The Hall extends through
the house. The Living-room, a large apartment adapted
to a good-sized family, is centrally situated, and protected
on every side from the direct rays of the sun ; it adjoins
the pleasant and shady verandas front and rear, both
being accessible through the folding windows, that open
like doors down to the floor. It communicates with the
hall through wide double doors, has a large closet and an
open fire. The Bedroom is of good dimensions, has three
windows opening to the verandas, and one side window.
The two closets are so arranged as to form an alcove to
the rear window. The ceiling of this alcove is arched
over, producing a very pleasant effect. An opening is
made near the ceiling into one of the flues of the adjoining chimney for ceiling ventilation. The Parlor (or Library) is situated in the most quiet part of the building,
where company may be entertained, or persons may en-
gage in reading or study, without disturbance from those
engaged in housework. Large windows open to the front
veranda, and other windows are provided at the side and
rear. A covered Passage-way leads from the rear hall
door to the food departments. These consist of a Dining-room, Kitchen, Store-room, and two Closets, and
to the rear of these is added a servant's Bedroom. The
dining-room and kitchen are each of ample size, with
windows arranged on opposite sides to admit a plentiful
supply of fresh air. A pump, sink, and two wash-tubs
are provided in the kitchen. The store-room and closets

are thoroughly shelved. If desirable, a china closet may be easily constructed at one side of the fire-place, into which one of the doors already provided would open.... SECOND STORY, (fig. 64.)—Hight of ceiling 9 feet. This may be divided into two or more rooms, as required, for bedrooms. The cross-partitions may be 8 feet high, admitting a free passage of air above them.... CONSTRUCTION.—Brick piers, placed 6 feet apart under all sills, are intended for the foundation. The remaining space is left unobstructed for the circulation of air. A cellar may be excavated, and walled up under the main house, with stairs leading to it from the rear veranda, under the main flight. In the estimate, provision is made for a regular frame of sawed timber, which should be framed and raised in a substantial manner. The siding for the main house and wings is of 6-inch pine clap-boards, laid 5 inches to the weather. The roofs of the main house and wings are laid with hemlock boards ; all other roofs and cornice projections are laid with inverted $1 \times 4^1/_2$-inch tongued and grooved pine flooring, and lastly covered with I C. charcoal tin, locked and soldered in the best manner. The cornices are constructed with wide projections, and have neat truss supports. The verandas are made with simple parts. The columns for the front are 7-inch boxed, with bases, and scrolled spandrels; for the rear of 3×4 joist with bases, and plain spandrels. The veranda plates and rafters are dressed for painting, and are left exposed to sight. The pediments shown on the front are of open work, to allow the warmed air from near the roofs to escape. The upper frame-work (plates and rafters) of the rear building are also planed, and left exposed to sight from the inside. The inclosing and partitions for this part are of $1 \times 4^1/_2$-inch pine tongued and grooved flooring, dressed on both sides, put on in a vertical manner, and nailed to the sills and plates ; $1^1/_4$-inch pine battens are put around the inside of the rooms at the proper hight for a chair-rail ($2^3/_4$ feet to the upper edge), and joined to the casings of the doors and windows of like materials, and all thoroughly nailed with "clinch" nails to the upright boarding. The roof is built as described for the verandas, is double pitch, and has sufficient spread to include the shed, making it a part of the same building. The kitchen chimney is built nearly in the center of this building, has a large open fire-place, and has a good hight above the roof. All floors are of $1 \times 4^1/_2$-inch tongued and grooved pine flooring, close laid and blind nailed. All rooms in the main building and wings are hard-finished upon two coats of brown mortar. All work usually painted has two coats of good paint. The roof-gutters are made as shown in Design V.... Estimate :

8,000 bricks in piers and chimneys, furnished and laid, at $12 per M.....	$96.00
550 yards plastering, at 28c. per yard..................	154.00
5,054 ft. timber, at $15 per M......	75.81

Sills, 4×8 in. 261 ft. long.	32 beams, 2×8 in. 21 ft. long.
Ties, 4×6 in. 261 ft. long.	4 posts, 4×7 in. 22 ft. long.
Plates, 4×6 in. 92 ft. long.	1 piazza sill, 3×8 in. 230 ft. long.
4 hips, 3×8 in. 17 ft. long.	1 piazza plate, 3×8 in. 206 ft. long.
56 beams, 2×8 in. 14 ft. long.	Piazza beams, 2×6 in. 384 ft. long.

50 joist, 3×4 in. 13 ft. long, at 16c. each........................... ...	8.00
300 wall-strips, 2×4 in. 13 ft. long, at 11c...................	33.00
370 siding (6-inch clap-boards), at 18c. each	66.60
170 hemlock boards, at 16c. each.................................	27.20
240 ft. cornice, bracketed, at 20c. per ft...........	48.00
208 ft. simple rear cornice, at 8c. per ft..... .'.........................	16.64
38 squares of tin, at $7 per square........................	266.00
6,000 ft. of 1×4¼ tongued and grooved flooring pine, at 3c. per ft........	180.00
24 piazza columns, complete, average at $1 each......	24.00
1 stairs, complete, $50; 31 windows, at $10, $310...........	360.00
20 doors. at $8, $160; 1 mantle, $50...................................	210.00
Sinks. pumps. and wash-tubs.......	22.00
Closet finish, $12 ; nails, $25.....	37.00
Painting, $100; carting. $20...	120.00
Boards for outside casings and incidentals...........	105.75
Carpenter's labor...	150.00
Total cost, complete. $2,000.00	

DESIGN XVI.

Fig. 65.—ELEVATION OF HOUSE.

A HOUSE COSTING $2,100.

This plan, embodying the principal characteristics of
a design I made several years ago, for the residence of
Mr. Arthur Waller, Newtown, L. I., has a homelike,
tasteful, and picturesque appearance—particularly now,
with its neatly laid-out grounds and grown up shrubbery,
which especially befit its *pointed style,* and demonstrate
the harmony that exists between these simple *cottage*
outlines, and rural surroundings. . It is thus adapted to
either a suburban or more retired country situation....
ELEVATION, (fig. 65.)—A noticeable peculiarity is the
earth finish around the foundation, which is simply util-
izing the earth from the cellar. This is banked against

the foundation, up to within six inches of the wood,
evenly graded at 45 degrees angle, and neatly covered
with closely laid turf. This conceals a roughly constructed foundation ; it insures more dryness of the cellar, and consequently of the whole house ; it guards the
cellar against extreme heat in summer, and frost in winter ; and it gives such a visible breadth of bottom as to
add to its appar-
ent strength.
This earth finish
around the foun-
dation is especial-
ly adapted to wet
or clayey soils,
where it is desir-
able to have the
cellar mostly
above ground ; at
the same time it
secures greater
elevation to the
whole building.
. . . . . There are
marked features
of dissimilarity
in the several

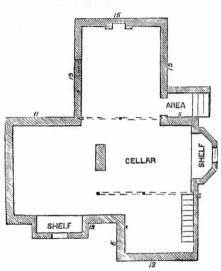

Fig 66.—PLAN OF CELLAR.

openings, and in the details of the exterior dressing, each
part being adapted to its special purpose, and so arranged
as to be in keeping with the general design ; it therefore
unites harmony and beauty. . . . CELLAR, (fig. 66.)—The
Cellar extends under the whole house ; clear hight $6\frac{1}{2}$
feet. The outside entrance to the cellar is by an area-
way, having stone steps and walls, with hatchway and
inside doors ; the hatchway doors, when closed, being
even with the sloping earth finish. . . . FIRST STORY, (fig.
67.)—Hight of ceiling $9\frac{1}{2}$ feet. The irregular outlines

of this plan contribute to the cheerfulness of the different apartments, by giving opportunity for the insertion of windows where they will command the most pleasing prospects. The principal entrance is from the porch through double doors to the spacious hall, which adjoins the parlor and dining-room. The Parlor has one bay and

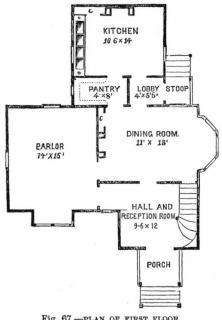

two plain windows, with large wall space for furniture and wall decoration. The Dining-room is conveniently arranged to connect with the principal hall, parlor, rear lobby, large pantry, or closet, and the cellar stairway, and has a large bay and one plain window. The Kitchen is planned to have a range, sink, pump, wash-

Fig. 67.—PLAN OF FIRST FLOOR.

tubs, and the usual pipes for cold and hot water, and is provided with two windows, situated in opposite sides of the room to give abundant light, and afford thorough ventilation ; a closet adjoins the chimney-breast, and a cupboard is put beneath the sink. The Pantry is of good dimensions, contiguous to both dining-room and kitchen, has a suitable window, and is furnished with shelving. The rear entrance is from the covered stoop to the rear

lobby, and from thence to either dining-room or kitchen.
.... SECOND STORY, (fig. 68.)—This story is reached by
a winding stairway from the principal hall, and contains
four good-sized chambers, a bath-room, five large closets,
and the needed passage-ways. The breast-walls are vertical to the height of $3^{1}/_{2}$ feet, and are continued upward
along the underside of the steep roof frame-work to the
ceiling, which is 8
feet high. The Bath-
room is p r o v i d e d
with a bath-tub and
seat - closet. T h e
Tank is 1 foot 8 in.
wide, 2 feet long,
and 3 feet deep, and
is placed in the closet
adjoining the bath-
room, at a hight of
2 feet above the floor,
and provided with a
neat-fitting lid. The
spaces above and be-
low the tank may be
used as a closet for
toweling, etc. The

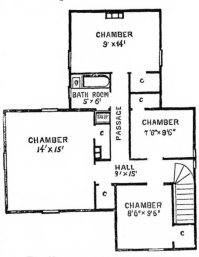

Fig. 68.—PLAN OF SECOND FLOOR.

interior location of this tank should insure it against
frost, so long as the house is occupied by the family....
CONSTRUCTION.—The excavations for the cellar are 2
feet deep, and the earth is used as above described. The
materials for the principal foundations may be of the
roughest stone, such as are commonly used in farm-fenc-
ing, and coarse mortar. Very little skill is required in
the construction of these walls, as only the last, or top
course, is seen from the outside, which should be laid to
a line, and levelled to receive the frame-work. The
exposed portions of the bay-window foundations **are**

constructed of brick laid in mortar, resting on stone-
work, and leaving an interior recess or shelf, as shown on
the cellar plan.   The cellar windows are of good dimensions, and situated where they will insure sufficient light,
and provide for the complete airing of the cellar.   An
opening should be left in one, or both of the chimneys,
near the cellar ceiling, having a continuous flue to the
top, which will be heated by contact with the fire-places
above when in use, and produce a draft that will exhaust
the poisonous vapors always generated in cellars, and
prevent them from rising through the house to contam-
inate the air of the living-rooms.   This cellar may be
easily and cheaply divided into separate apartments by
rough planking or otherwise, if ever desirable.   The rear
portion might be readily converted into a laundry, where
the wash-tubs, with their accompanying pipes, might be
placed, leaving more kitchen room, and relieving it of
the steam and general disturbance of the ever-recurring
washing days.   Large durable posts are placed in the cellar, resting on large flat stones that have been embedded
in the cellar bottom, as supports for the 4×8-inch girders, shown on the cellar plan by the dotted lines.   By
the estimate, it will be seen that very little timber is used
in the frame-work, of which the sills and beams comprise
the heavier parts.   I would enforce the importance of
having the frame fitted and secured together in a substantial manner.   The beams should be bridged as described for Design XVII.... The exterior sides of the
frame-work are designed to be inclosed with double boarding, with an intermediate lining of tarred felting. The first
covering should be milled to even thicknesses, and put on
horizontally and double nailed to each stud.   The felting is
next applied in whole width strips, running from the sill to
the plate.   The water-table and window-frames are next put
in their places, after which the final covering of tongued
and grooved sheathing is put on vertically, with the lower

ends neatly fitted to the water-table, and the upper ends covered with a 10-inch board forming a frieze to the cornice. The siding should then be painted one coat in a thorough manner, when battens of 1¹/₂ inch "half round" (previously painted both sides) are firmly nailed over the joints of the sheathing. The windows are all arranged for 1¹/₂-inch sash, hung to iron weights with good cord, and neatly cased and moulded on the inside; outside blinds are intended for each window above the cellar. The cornices are constructed in the simplest manner, and the perforated barges and finials are made as indicated by the elevation, and placed near the extremity of the gable cornices, from which ever-varying shadows are made against the building, producing the most delicate and pleasing effects. It is purposely intended that the roofs of the principal building, porch, stoop, bay, and dormer windows, shall have sufficient pitch for shingling . . . . .

The character of the balance of the work may be inferred from the estimate which is given in detail.—ESTIMATE :

61 yards excavation, at 20c. per yard	$12.20
1,278 ft. stone foundation. complete. at 12c. per ft	153.36
5,000 brick for bays and chimneys. furnished and laid, at $12 per M	60.00
30 ft. stone steps and coping. at 30c. per ft	9.00
660 yards 3-coat plastering. complete, at 28c. per yard	184.80
3,526 ft. timber. at $15 per M	52.89

1 sill, 4×8 in. 151 ft. long.	13 beams. 3×8 in.. 22 ft. long.
10 posts, 4×6 in. 13 ft. long.	19 beams, 3×8 in. 16 ft. long.
1 plate. 4×6 in. 136 ft. long.	15 beams, 3×8 in. 15 ft. long.
4 valleys, 3×7 in. 17 ft. long.	1 beam. 3×7 in. 80 ft. long.
1 girder, 4×8 in. 16 ft. long.	50 rafters, 3×4 in. 13 ft. long.

300 wall-strips. 2×4×13. at 11c. each	33.00
200 sheathing, 9 in.. at 18c. each	36.00
100 lbs. tarred felting, at 5c. per lb	5.00
200 tongued and grooved sheathing, at 28c. each	56.00
200 battens. at 6c. each	12.00
Materials in cornices and water-table	38.00
325 shingling-lath, 1¼×2×13, at 6c. each	19.50
60 bunches shingles. at $1.50 per bunch	90.00
177 flooring. 1¼×9¼ in., at 25c. each	44.25
2 stoops (front and rear). complete	80.00
2 bay-windows (with blinds). complete	100.00
10 plain windows (with blinds) complete. at $12 each	120.00
4 dormer windows (with blinds). complete, at $20 each	80.00
3 cellar windows. complete. at $6 each	18.00
Stairs. complete. $75: 24 doors. complete. at $8 each. $192	267.00
3 mantles. complete. $20. $10. and $6	36.00
Shelving. etc., $12: nails, $18; painting, $110	140.00
Plumbing and range. complete. $222 70; cartage, average 1 mile, $25.	247.70
Carpenter's labor. not included above	150.00
For contingencies	55.30
Total cost, complete	**$2,100.00**

5

D E S I G N   X V I I.

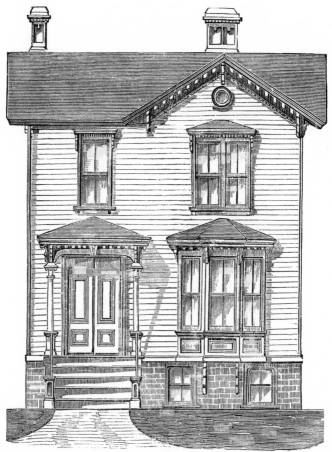

Fig. 69.—ELEVATION OF FRONT OF HOUSE.

A HOUSE COSTING $2,200.

These plans are for a full two-story house, that will embrace the merits of the most economical form of construction (having a floor measurement of 24×28, nearly

square),with symmetry of style,and containing a very commodious and convenient interior arrangement.   The ELE-
VATION (fig. 69), has marked features of simplicity and refinement, with sufficient diversity of parts to give variety
and grace, without pretentious display.   We invariably
recommend high foundations for houses of this character ; of course a foot in hight at the bottom will add a
foot to the hight of
the whole, imparting
a better appearance
externally, and on ac-
count of the better
ventilation thereby
afforded to the cellar,
adds greatly to the
healthfulness of the
interior of the whole
house.   Additional
steps will be required
to the stoops, but the
cost of these are com-
pensated by deduc-
tions in the excava-
tion for the cellar,
and stone steps to the
area. The large porch

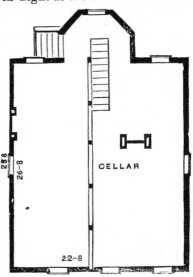

Fig. 70.—PLAN OF CELLAR.

and double doors, the bay and other windows, each dis-
tinctive in themselves, and adapted to their places, similar only in conformity of character, are so proportioned
as to harmonize with each other with pleasing effect.
The pediments of the roof are so arranged that each
"face" of the building will have very nearly the same
appearance of outline.   The main cornice projects two
feet beyond the frame-work of the house, and is supported
by large trusses ; all other cornices and window-caps have
proportionate projections, insuring heavy shadows, giving

relief and finish to the whole.... CELLAR, (fig. 70.)—
Excavations for this cellar are made 2 feet 6 inches below
the general surface of the ground. The Foundation-
walls, Chimneys, Girder - supports, and rear Area-
walls are built as described for De-
sign XII., after which the earth
is graded around, and up against
the foundation, so as to give such
slope as will turn the water away
from the house and walks, leaving
the foundation 4 feet above the final
grade..... FIRST STORY, (fig. 71)
—This story con-
tains the principal
hall, parlor, din-
ing or living-room,
kitchen, rear lob-
by, three closets,
and private stairs.
The principal
Hall is entered
from the front

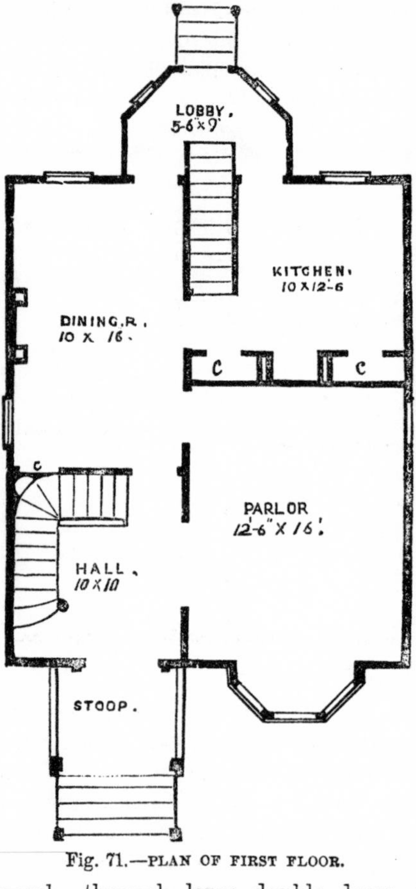

Fig. 71.—PLAN OF FIRST FLOOR.

porch, through large double doors, is square (10×10
feet), and contains the principal stairs, which are built
with a quarter circle and niche nearly in the center of
their height, as described in Design XII.   This hall

connects with the parlor through double doors ; this will be found to give an impression of amplitude that would scarcely be expected in a house of this size. The Parlor has a large bay-window, finished with elliptical arch and ornamental corbels, and a marble mantle. The Dining-room is intended as the living-room of the family, and communicates with each room and hall of the first story ; has a closet under the front stairs, and has a marble mantle. The Kitchen is provided with a large range, two closets, sink, with cold and hot water, and closet underneath, and communicates with the dining-room, lobby, and cellar stairway. The rear entrance to this story is through the lobby, which

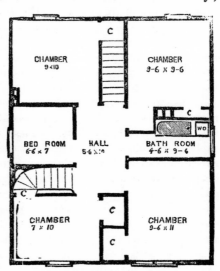

Fig. 72.—PLAN OF SECOND FLOOR.

has two small windows. The private stairs are arranged to start from the rear lobby.... SECOND STORY, (fig. 72.)—The manner in which this story is divided into rooms very much resemble a "double" house, the hall being nearly in the center of the house, and the rooms at either side : contains hall, two stairways, six rooms, and five closets. The hall is 5 ft. 6 in. ×10 ft., and has seven doors leading from it to the different rooms and private stairway. Many persons require a "study"; the room directly above the principal hall is best adapted for such purpose, has a large closet, and is most convenient to the stairs. The door to this room should have ground glass upper panels, to admit light to the hall. The Bath-room is provided with French bath-tub, seat-closet, and wash-basin. The soil-pipe from this story will be concealed by passing down inside one of the kitchen closets. Marble shelves, resting on stucco trusses, are intended for each of the four principal rooms of this story.... GENERAL DETAILS.—It is intended that all the work should be done in a workmanlike and substantial manner, of good materials, as indicated in the estimate. All the principal timber is framed together, and raised in the usual manner, and secured with hard-wood pins. The enclosing should be dressed, of thoroughly seasoned materials, and nailed with 10*d*. nails. The cornices are ornamented with bold panelled brackets and dentil courses. Each gable is provided with a circular ventilator. All roofs are covered with charcoal tin, laid on rough boards, and have gutters as described for Design V., at a cost of 10 cts. per running foot. The columns of the front porch are turned, and have ornamental caps and square pedestals. The stoop-rail is 5 inches wide, and the balusters are scroll-sawed, of $1\frac{1}{2}$-inch pine plank. The trusses under the bay-window are large, scroll-sawed, and ornamental. The flooring should be thoroughly dried, close-laid, and double-nailed to each beam with 10*d*. nails. While laying the floor (having reached the center of the span of the beams), a row of cross-bridging should be put in, in a strong manner. In this way, the *inequalities* of the upper surfaces of the beams, which are always more or less sprung, will be brought *into line* by the flooring, and each piece of bridging will receive its relative proportion of the weight. The tarred paper is next inserted between the outside studding, in the manner described for Design XI., which is much cheaper than "brick-filling," and for many reasons more desirable. The cen-

tral partitions, that carry the principal weight, should be
studded strongly of 4-inch materials, or wall-strips set
edgeways. All closet, stair, and cross partitions may be
set of 2-inch materials, or wall-strips set flatways. This
latter method saves nearly one-half of the space taken by
the partitions, which may be added to the size of the
rooms, where it frequently happens that a few inches becomes a matter of importance. The second-story ceiling
timbers are of wall-strips, put 12 inches from centers,
and a flooring of rough boards is laid over a part, to make
room for storage, etc. All sash are $1^1/_2$ inches thick, and
have second quality French glass in them, and are hung
with iron weights. We think there is a good opportunity for improvement in the manufacture of window
sashes, making them air-tight, and suggest inserting the
necessary rubber strips near their edges, and especially in
the lips of the check-rail—this would effectually shut
out all drafts of air, and make the unsightly and imprac-
ticable "weather-strip" unnecessary. All stairs should
have $1^1/_4$ strings and treads, and $^7/_8$ risers, and should be
so housed, glued, and keyed, as to make them solid ;
squeaky stairs are abominable, and even when assured of
their safety, one feels an instinctive suspicion of danger,
and will look for treachery in every part of the house.
Black walnut panelled newel, moulded rail, and fluted
balusters, are intended for the principal flight of stairs.
Setting the niche is a part of the stair-builder's work,
and should always be included in his estimate for stairs
of this character. The trimming of the hall, dining-
room, and parlor, are of clear pine, the architraves are 8
inches wide, and "double-moulded," with panelled back
to each window. Base 7-inch and moulded. All other
rooms have 5-inch "single trim," with back moulding,
and base to match. All doors panelled and moulded ; all
room-doors have mortise locks, and closet-doors have
rim-locks, all with brass bolts and keys ; knobs and

escutcheons of porcelain, and all saddles are of hard-wood. All parts of this house that are usually painted should have two coats of paint of the best materials, and of such colors as shall suit the owner. All hard-wood, such as the stair-rail, bath-room finish, and saddles, should have two coats of linseed-oil.... COST.—Contractors everywhere differ in their estimates for work of any kind. These differences are sometimes the result of some peculiar circumstance, but most generally they arise through some misapprehension of fact ; either the plans are incomprehensible, or the description of them ambiguous, leading to a variety of interpretations, and consequently a variety of prices, some of which are too low, and some too high. The low man who usually *proposes* to do the best work, and the most of it, gets the job, and executes the work in accordance with his preconceived ideas, gets his money, and leaves the owner in possession of something he did not expect. No one can know the extent and character of the work better than the projector of them, who should be equally qualified to give exact estimates of quantities and cost of everything connected with their thorough development and execution, and thus truly fulfill his mission as the architect of the works. Cost is one of the most interesting features in any project, and no plan is hardly worth considering that does not comprehend in some way the expense of its execution. Builders and others interested in such plans, will appreciate the detailed estimates, as furnishing the key to the whole plan, supplying the needed information as to the real quality and character of the work.—ESTIMATE :

62 yards excavation, at 20c. per yard...	$12.40
13,000 hard brick, furnished and laid, at $12 per M	156.00
700 yards lath and plastering, at 28c. per yard	196.00
32 ft. stone steps, at 40c. per ft.	12.80
24 ft. stone sills, at 30c. per ft.	7.20
2,300 ft. of timber, at $15 per M	34.50

2 sills, 4×7 in. 24 ft. long.	2 plates, 4×6 in. 24 ft. long.
2 sills. 4×7 in. 28 ft. long.	2 plates, 4×6 in. 28 ft. long.
4 posts, 4×7 in. 20 ft. long.	1 girt, 4×8 in. 28 ft. long.
2 ties, 4×6 in. 24 ft. long.	30 beams, 3×7 in. 24 ft. long.
2 ties, 4×6 in. 28 ft. long.	4 valleys, 3×7 in. 12 ft. long.

400 wall-strips, 2×4 in. 13 ft. long. at 11c. each	$44.00
230 novelty clear siding-boards. at 28c. each	64.40
175 lbs. tarred paper, at 5c. per lb	8.75
150 tongued and grooved flooring. at 28c. each	42.00
130 hemlock roof-boards. 16c. each	20.80
12 squares of tin roofing, at $7 per square	84.00
156 ft. gutters and leaders, at 10c. per ft	15.60
104 ft. cornice, at 40c. per ft	41.60
1 bay-window (with blinds). complete	75.00
12 plain windows (with blinds). complete, at $16 each	192.00
8 cellar windows. complete, at $4 each	32.00
1 stoop (except tin as above), complete	70.00
27 doors, complete, at $9 each, $243; 3 stairs, complete, $70	313.00
2 marble mantles, and 4 shelves on trusses	50.00
Range. plumbing. sink, bath, water-closet, and pump	314.55
Corner-boards, base. and shelving, $32.50; nails, $20	52.50
Cartage, average one mile	20.00
Capenter's labor. not included above, $200; painting, $100.	300.00
Incidentals	40.90
Total cost, complete	$2,200.00

DESIGN XVIII.

A SOUTHERN HOUSE COSTING $2,200.

This plan of a simple, yet genteel Southern house, embraces ample interior accommodation for the wants of a good-sized family. It has an abundance of outside verandas and artificial shade, and may be constructed at a very moderate cost.... EXTERIOR, (fig. 73.)—The style is adapted to the Middle and Southern States, because of its elevation and airiness, the overhanging projections of its roof, and the facility with which wings or verandas may be added. The Tower is a conspicuous feature, and though without any special ornamentation, it gives an expression of unity and completeness to the whole structure. The Verandas on every side afford protection from the sun. Many persons prefer disconnected verandas (as shown in figs. 73 and 75), with open ends to the roofs for the escape of the heated air that would otherwise be retained in them. Moreover, disconnected verandas prevent the annoyance arising from the noise made by children who are fond of running and playing upon them. .... CELLAR, (fig. 74.)—This is under the kitchen wing only; is 6½ feet deep, has two windows, an outside en-

trance with stone steps, and a stairway leading to the
rear entry of the first floor.... FIRST STORY, (fig. 75.)—
Hight of ceiling in the main house, 11 feet, and in the
wing 9 feet. The entrance Hall, nearly square, and en-

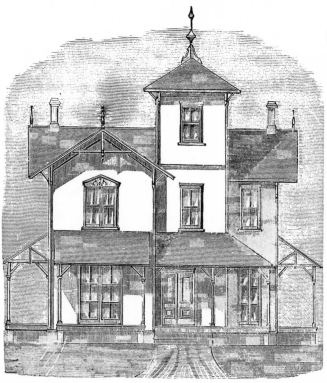

Fig. 73.—VIEW OF EXTERIOR OF A SOUTHERN HOUSE.

tered from the front piazza through double doors, contains the main stairs, and communicates with the parlor
and dining-room. Each of these apartments communicates with the library through large sliding-doors. The
windows to these rooms open to the floor, and are pro-

tected on the outside by the verandas. The front parlor window is 6½ feet wide, with the sashes arranged to slide in pockets at either side, by which means the parlor is apparently pro-longed to, and may be used with the veranda. Each of the large rooms has fireplaces and marble mantles. The closet for the dining-room is under the main stairs. The Kitchen is in the rear wing, and separated from the main house by the rear lobby and the pantry; it has a good-sized double window at each side, a large pantry, and a fireplace. In the rear entry are stairways leading to the second story and to the cellar..... SECOND STORY, (fig. 76.)

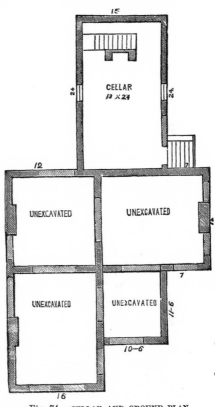

Fig. 74.—CELLAR AND GROUND PLAN.

—Hight of ceilings in main house, 9 feet, and in the wing 7 feet. It is divided into six chambers, besides halls and closets. The three larger Chambers have fireplaces with marble shelves, and two windows in each. The window in the small chamber is placed near the ceiling, above the kitchen roof. The two Chambers in in the wing are intended as servants rooms, and have no communication with the main house.....TOWER AND ATTIC.—The Tower has an inclosed stairway, with a door at the foot.

Fig. 75.—PLAN OF FIRST FLOOR.

The main roof finish at the rear of the tower is leveled even with the main ridge, inclosing the intervening space; this affords room for a door leading from the tower to the attic. This story is thoroughly floored, and has small windows in each gable, and is useful as a place for storage. In cases of necessity, a portion of this attic may be used for bedrooms.... CONSTRUCTION.

—The Cellar excavations are made in the ground $4\frac{1}{2}$ feet deep, and for the underpinning of the main house one foot. The loose earth is used in grading, raising the surface immediately surrounding the foundation 8 inches. The foundation walls are 8 inches thick, of hard brick and good mortar. The cellar walls are $6\frac{1}{2}$ feet high, and the underpinning 3 feet 2 inches high, leaving an exposed surface 18 inches high at completion. Only the portions of the foundation plan, shown darker in the plan, fig. 74, are walled, the intervening spaces being left open for the free circulation of air. The general character of the materials to be used in the construction of this house (a large por-

tion of which is milled, and manufactured ready for use,) may be inferred from the appended estimate. The manner of putting these materials together is of great importance, and should be entrusted only to skillful and thorough workmen. The details of the exterior finish are so plain, that the work of "getting out" the several parts may be done by the mechanics employed in building, without recourse to the scroll-saw or

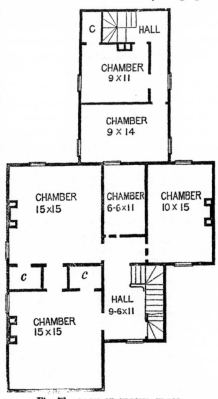

Fig. 76.—PLAN OF SECOND FLOOR.

carver. The truss-work of the cornices, and the open frame-work, and columns of the verandas, are of dressed timber, and stop-chamfered. All the roofs have sufcient pitch to allow the use of shingles, which are much lighter and cooler than slate or metal. Veranda roofs so

constructed do not reflect so much heat into the chamber
windows as others, which is important in a warm climate.....VENTILATION.—Large window openings, with
easy working sashes, are provided, and afford the best
means of changing the air of any apartment. The chimneys are large, and have open fire-places, and ventilating
side-flues with registers near the ceilings. These openings, which should never be closed, will be found to afford
satisfactory ventilation. During seasons of extreme heat,
the tower may be made to serve as a general ventilator,
by lowering the upper sashes, and opening all the doors
leading to it. The following estimate includes everything
necessary to complete this building in a thorough manner, at prices now ruling in the vicinity of New York.—
ESTIMATE :

61 yards excavation, at 20c. per yard	$12.20
15,000 bricks, furnished and laid, at $12 per M	180.00
26 ft. stone steps and sills, at 30c. per ft	7.80
700 yards plastering, at 28c. per yard	196.00
6,112 ft. of timber, at $15 per M	91.68

Sills, 4×8 in. 247 ft. long.
1 tie, 4×6 in. 247 it. long.
1 plate, 4×6 in. 247 ft. long.
7 posts, 4×7 in. 22 ft. long.
4 posts, 4×7 in. 34 ft. long.
1 ridge, 2×7 in. 40 ft. long.
1 ridge, 2×7 in. 30 ft. long.

78 beams, 2×8 in. 16 ft. long.
34 beams, 2×8 in. 15 ft. long.
39 beams, 2×7 in. 16 ft. long.
15 beams, 2×7 in. 11 ft. lodg.
1 piazza, 2×7 in. 375 ft. long.
2 valleys, 3×8 in. 16 ft. long.

100 joist, 3×4 in. 13 ft. long, at 16c. each	16.00
400 wall-strips, 2×4 in. 13 ft. long, at 11c. each	44.00
420 siding (6¼ in. wide 13 ft. long, at 26c. each	109.20
Materials in cornices and verandas	40.00
120 hemlock boards (for main house), at 15c. each	18.00
236 pine boards for roofing, 4¼×13, at 18c. each	42.48
67 bunches shingles, at $1.50 per bunch	100.50
Finial on tower	8.00
168 Flooring for verandas, 4¼ in. wide, at 20c. each	33.60
360 flooring for inside, 9½ in. wide, at 26c. cach	93.60
Stairs, $70 ; closet finish, $20	90.00
2 cellar windows, complete, at $6 each	12.00
28 windows, at $10, $280 ; 32 doors, at $9, $288	568.00
3 mantles, $25 each, $75; 3 shelves, $6 each, $18	93.00
224 ft. gutters and leaders, at 8c. per ft	17.92
Nails, $22; painting, $125 : carting, $25	172.00
Carpenter's labor, not included above	200.00
Incidentals	54.02
Total cost, complete	$2,200.00

DESIGN XIX.

Fig. 77.—FRONT VIEW OF HOUSE.

A STONE HOUSE, COSTING $2,500.

This plan has many features to commend it as an economical country house. It is similar in many respects to Design XXVII., having an equal breadth of front, and is constructed of like substantial materials. The arrangement of the several parts, however, are more regular and compact, and embrace accommodations for a good-sized family.... EXTERIOR, (fig. 77.)—At first sight, the reader will perceive the perfect balance apparent in the outlines and details of the front. Variety is also an especial feature, resulting from the pleasing diversity and systematic distribution of the prominent parts. The site has much effect upon the appearance of any building. This house should have a commanding position to afford such views as would seem to be expected from its broad and generous windows. Health and happiness being

largely dependent on the situation, it is important to
select a position having a natural drainage, and therefore
more likely to be surrounded with pure wholesome air.
.... CELLAR, (fig. 78.)—Hight $6\frac{1}{2}$ feet. The plain engraving saves the need of further explanation. The ceiling is smoothly " laid off" with one coat of plaster, and
the walls are flush-pointed, so that the whole interior
may be whitewashed whenever it shall be desirable to
lighten or sweeten the cellar.... FIRST STORY, (fig. 79.)—

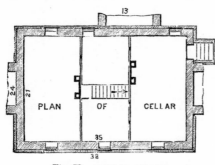

Fig. 78.—PLAN OF CELLAR.

As is suggested
by the exterior,
system and order
are prominent
features in the in-
terior arrange-
ment. The main
entrance is
through double
doors. The prin-
cipal hall is cen-
tral and roomy,
and contains the open and balustered stairway to the
second story. The two principal rooms are of equal
size, with outlooks front and rear. The Parlor has
a pleasant bay or plant window, arranged to be shut
off, when desirable, by large sash doors. This window
has no floor, but is cemented around its sides below the
floor-line, to secure dryness to the walls, and is filled with
earth wherein plants may be grown. The thick masonry surrounding this plant-bed will secure it from frost.
The temperature required to make the parlor comfortable
will be sufficient for the plants, while the strong sunlight
will insure their vigorous growth. A mirror may be
placed on the mantle opposite this window, arranged to
reflect its contents, and make a most cheerful picture.—
The Living-room is a convenient apartment, in easy com-

munication with the front and rear entrances, the wood-house, and cellar-stairs, passing down under the front hall stairs. It has a large pantry, and is provided with a range, sink, stationary wash-tubs, water, and waste-pipes. The importance of having cold and hot water always ready should not be overlooked. Very much of the drudgery of housework in the country consists in draw-ing and carrying water, and be-sides, it general-ly happens that when water is most wanted, the vessels are empty, necessi-tating great in-convenience and frequent dis-tress.—The Bed-room is situated between the par-lor and living-

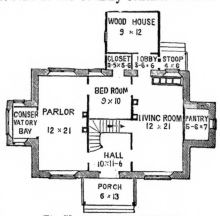

Fig. 79.—PLAN OF FIRST FLOOR.

room, and communicates with both, and has a good-sized closet. This apartment may be used as a sewing-room, where such work need not be put away every time it is laid down for a moment. The Wood-house at the rear is constructed of light materials, and serves as a fuel and utensil room.... SECOND STORY, (fig. 80.)—This story is divided into five chambers, a hall, and seven closets. Each room is entered directly from the hall, obviating the too frequent necessity of passing through one room to reach another. Closets are a necessity to any well ordered household ; their uses are so numerous that it is hardly possible to provide too many..... REMARKS ON CONSTRUCTION.—The element of durability is an import-ant quality of this structure, avoiding the necessity and

expense of frequent repairs. The exterior walls are constructed of stone and brick, as described in Design
XXVII. Care should be taken to make these walls perfectly solid and thorough. The mortar used should be of
the best lime, and coarse, sharp sand. Such mortar im-
proves with age, always increasing in hardness and
strength. The brick corner-work may be laid in dark or
blue mortar with good effect in subduing the strong con-
trasts in color.

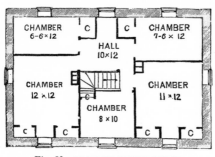

Fig. 80 —PLAN OF SECOND FLOOR.

Interior plaster-
ing should never
be applied direct-
ly to the stone-
work. Such walls
do not readily
conform to the
sudden changes
of the surround-
ing temperature,
and are rendered
damp and unwholesome from the moisture of the air being
condensed upon them. They should be furred off, leaving an air-space between the stone-work and plastering,
through the whole hight of the wall, and opening into
the spaces between the rafters of the roof. Side-walls
constructed in this manner afford a most comfortable
interior, having a more equal temperature than is possible in the usual frame building, and neither the severe
cold of winter, nor the extreme heat of summer, is immediately felt within. The chimneys are of hard brick;
their interior location insures a great saving of fuel, as
the heat that is radiated from them greatly assists in
warming the house. The principal roofs are covered with
dark slate. "Keystone" and "Chapman" are good
qualities, and are mostly used in this vicinity; they have
good color, and do not fade. A good effect is produced

by clipping the exposed corners of about one-third of the slate, in a uniform manner, and laying them in belts of five or six courses each across the roof.

Estimate of the Cost :

111 yards excavation, at 20c. per yard................................	$22.20
171 perches stone-work, at $2.75 per perch........................	470.25
103 ft. stone sills and steps, at 30c. per ft......................	30.90
2,000 bricks in angles, etc., at $12 per M., laid.................	24.00
4,000 bricks in chimneys, at $12 per M., laid.....................	48.00
660 yards plastering, at 28c. per yard............................	184.80
80 yards plastering in ceiling of cellar, at 20c. per yard........	16.00
3,367 ft. of timber, at $15 per M.................................	50.50

2 girders, 4×8 in. 32 ft. long.	44 beams, 3×8 in. 13 ft. long.
4 plates, 4×8 in. 11 ft. long.	22 beams, 3×8 in. 11 ft. long.
2 purlins, 4×8 in. 38 ft. long.	40 rafters, 2×5 in. 19 ft. long.
1 ridge, 2×6 in. 29 ft. long.	4 valleys, 3×7 in. 21 ft. long.
1 ridge, 2×6 in. 22 ft. long.	18 collars, 1¼×5 in. 14 ft. long.

230 wall-strips, at 11c. each.....................................	25.30
130 furring strips, at 6c. each...................................	7.80
Anchors, of tire iron, $3 ; cornice materials, $30.	33.00
300 shingling-lath, at 6c. each...................................	18.00
Rear wing, exclusive of tin. complete............................	100.00
20 squares of slate, at $9 per square............................	180.00
32 hemlock boards, at 16c. each..................................	5.12
3½ squares of tin, at $7 per square..............................	24.50
60 ft. of leaders and gutters, at 10c. per ft....................	6.00
213 flooring, 8 inch, at 25c. each...............................	53.25
Stairs, complete...	70.00
Piazza and stoop, exclusive of tin, complete.....................	80.00
6 cellar windows, complete, at $5 each...........................	30.00
17 plain windows, complete, at $10 each..........................	170.00
4 dormer windows, complete, at $18 each..........................	72.00
27 doors, complete, at $9 each...................................	243.00
4 mantles, 2 marble and 2 wooden, complete.......................	62.00
Closet finish, complete..	18.00
Range and plumbing, complete.....................................	150.00
Nails, $14 : painting, $60 ; cartage, $15........................	89.00
Carpenter's labor, not included above............................	125.00
Incidentals..	91.38
Total cost, complete...	**$2,500.00**

DESIGN XX.

A COUNTRY HOUSE, COSTING $2,600.

This plan is somewhat similar in style and materials to Design XXIV. The changes here indicated adapt it to a more southern climate, such as larger window openings, more piazzas, and placing the domestic rooms at the *rear* of the main building.... EXTERIOR, (fig. 81.)—"Double front" houses (as those having their front entrance in the center are usually called), may face any point of compass,

and are adapted to almost any situation. They appear
best when located at sufficient distance from the road to
allow extended, neatly laid-out approaches, and thus give
an air of retirement.... CELLAR, (fig. 82.)—Hight, 7

Fig. 81.—ELEVATION OF FRONT OF HOUSE.

feet. Full size of the main building, with window openings on every side.... FIRST STORY, (fig. 83.)—Hight of
ceilings in main house, 11 feet; in the wing, 9 feet. The
apartments embraced in the main house are unusually
large, airy, and pleasant. All the windows open down
to the floor, and are protected from sun and rain by the
piazza. The Hall has a wide entrance leading from the
piazza, and contains the principal flight of stairs. The

occupy them.   Unlike the villager, the farmer has ample
road front, and his house should be so arranged as to

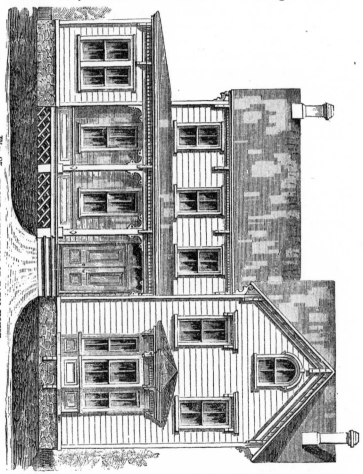

Fig. 85.—FRONT ELEVATION OF FARM HOUSE.

secure the most pleasant outlook from the living-rooms.
..... EXTERIOR, (fig. 85.)—Farm houses usually stand
disconnected and apart from other buildings, and should

6

have outlines that will best adapt them to the conditions
that are otherwise manifest in the location. This plan
is intended for an eastern frontage, where it would face
the morning sun, when the principal and broader portions
of the building, at the right, would be doubly valuable as
a shield to ward off the northern winds from the parts of
the house most used by the occupants. (By reversing

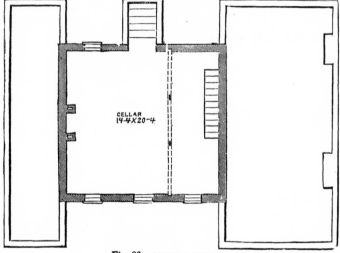

CELLAR
14-4X20-4

Fig. 86.—PLAN OF CELLAR.

the plan it would be equally adapted to the opposite, or
easterly side of a road.) It is intended that the body of
the house shall be set at least two feet above the ground;
this gives opportunity for good-sized cellar-windows, that
will admit light, and afford good openings for cellar ventilation, and also secure the frame-work of the building
against moisture from the ground. Such moisture, if
allowed, will cause decay of the sills and other principal
timbers, and is sure to percolate upward into the house,
filling it with unwholesome vapors. The variety of the
general outlines as shown in the elevation are calculated

to impart a cheerful and lively appearance always desirable in a country home, and very pleasant to the passer-
by. The ridged roofs, with their spreading gables and
ample projections, are features of frankness in which
there is no attempt at concealment or imitation. The
bay-windows, wide entrance, and spacious piazza, are

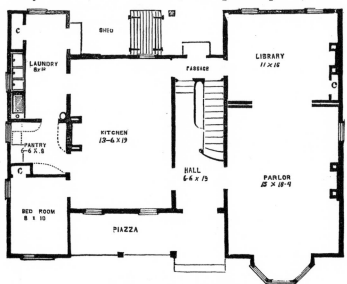

Fig. 87.—PLAN OF FIRST STORY.

each expressive of liberality and refinement. The extreme
simplicity of the details, and methods of construction,
devoid of all ostentatious display, clearly express the purpose of the building, and commend it to the consideration
of all who are interested in rural house building.....
FOUNDATION, (fig. 86.)—In most locations stone are
abundant; our estimate comprehends the building of the
foundation-walls of rough, broken stone, laid in coarse
mortar, and neatly pointed where exposed to sight. Any
man who is at all familiar with the most ordinary stone-

work, such as building "wall" fences, could build these foundations acceptably; they should be laid up 18 inches thick, and flush with the outside of the frame-work of the building. Our plan shows a cellar under the central part of the building only, which should be 7 feet deep; this cellar will be found sufficiently spacious for the uses of most families, but may be enlarged if desirable. One

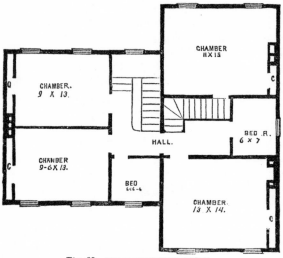

Fig. 88.—PLAN OF SECOND STORY.

of the "wise sayings" we heard in youth was, "always build your cellar under the whole house." Unless there are ample cellars under the barns, the house-cellar is never too large. In this case, it will be but little extra cost and labor to take out the earth, and carry the foundations down. The walls provided would do most of this, and then we have ample cellars for all wants, and have room to partition off fruit and vegetable rooms, the former of which need to be much cooler than the latter, if one would keep fruit well. The side-walls of the area are built of the same materials as the cellar-walls, with

the stone steps inserted while building. The foundations
shown on the plan where no cellar is required, are built
of the same materials, laid in trenches, which have been
excavated 18 inches wide, and 2 feet deep. The chimney
foundations should be started and laid up with the other
walls. A very effectual ventilation may be provided from
the cellar by arranging an opening that shall lead to the
left-hand flue of the kitchen chimney ; this flue will be
warmed by contact with the range when in use, and a
strong draft will be made, which will exhaust the damp,
foul odors so common in deep cellars. It will be observed
that the cellar is protected from the extreme changes of
outward temperature by the walls and spaces at each side,
and by the partial coverings in front and rear.... FIRST
STORY, (fig. 87.)—This story is divided into three large
and three small rooms, and hall. By this plan, the
kitchen is intended as the living-room of the family, and
is so arranged as to be the most *convenient and pleasant
room in the house;* has large windows front and rear,
which will admit an abundance of light, and afford an
outlook each way. A large range is placed in the fire-
place, with a water-back connecting with the boiler in
the laundry. The clock and lamp-shelf is placed on the
opposite side of the room from the fire-place : *should
never be over it.* Adjoining the kitchen, and connected
with it, is a pantry, containing shelving, drawers, and a
wash-tray, with cold and hot water. The Laundry, or *work-
room,* is arranged to connect directly with the kitchen and
pantry, and leads to the rear outside door. This room
is fitted up so that the principal kitchen-work may be
done in it, with great facility, and with few steps, and
contains a closet, sink, pump, wash-tubs, tank, and
boiler. The hight of the ceiling in this room is 10 feet
in the clear. The Tank (not shown in the drawings), is
situated close up to the ceiling, above the pantry door, is
8 feet long, 3 feet wide, and 2 feet deep. The boiler is

of copper, 40-gallon capacity, and is placed directly in the rear of the kitchen chimney. The sink and wash-tubs are shown on the plan, and are to be provided with cold and hot water. The force-pump is placed next to the sink, under the tank—by this method but little plumbing is required, and a very perfect and satisfactory arrangement is secured. The boiler keeps the tempera-ture of this room sufficiently warm to prevent damage to the pipes from frost. The Bedroom also adjoins the kitchen, and has a closet for clothing, and two windows. The principal Hall, included in the central building, is entered through large double doors from the front piazza, and connects through doors with the parlor, kitchen, and back passage, and contains the principal stairs, which are of easy "platform" construction. The Parlor has a large bay-window, marble mantle, and adjoins the library through large sliding-doors. The Library has a marble mantle, and closet, and connects with the back passage at the rear of the principal stairs. The Front Piazza has its ends sheltered by the projections at each side, and is arranged to require but two columns. If desirable at any time, a part of this piazza can be enclosed with sash at very little expense, which would provide a very conven-ient conservatory for plants and flowers. The rear "shed" is provided with a roof and columns, but has no wooden floor. It is intended that the grounds around the rear of the central building shall be graded well up, say within a foot of the rear door-sills, so as to require but a single step, or large flat stone, to each door. The outside cellar doors would be made to lay even with the final grade, and hung to the coping-stones of the area-walls, and the remaining space paved or flagged with stone. When once properly done, the finish of this char-acter will last a lifetime without trouble, while wood-work could never be satisfactory, and would often require re-newal. Whenever the cellar doors are opened, they are

hooked up against the columns, where they form a railing, or guard, to prevent the usual danger of an open
hatchway.... The SECOND STORY (fig. 88), has a hall,
four large and three small chambers, with four closets, and
stairway leading to the attic. Each of the large Chambers has two windows, and a ventilating register in the
flue of the chimney adjoining. All these rooms have full
hight ceilings, and are not so close to the roof as to be
affected by their absorbed heat of summer, but have complete square ceilings, with large air-spaces between them
and the roofs. The Attic of the principal building is
completely floored, and has windows in each gable or
pediment, and may be used for storage, drying clothes in
stormy weather, and for many other purposes.... CON-
STRUCTION.—The estimate appended indicates the kind
and quantity of materials used, which will be found to be
such as are now most generally adopted for buildings of
this character. The work is very simple, and may be
executed by the simplest methods. Information concern-
ing the application and uses of the "felting" may be
found in Design XI. We have before suggested that
"there are circumstances that would justify the building
of one part of a house first." Should it be desirable, the
central portion of this house could be built first, and
would be found quite sufficient as the dwelling house of a
small family, and the remainder added afterwards as required.... ESTIMATE.—The following estimate has been
carefully compiled, and may be relied on for quantities,
etc. Prices vary in different localities, but the figures
here given form a good basis of calculation :

65 yards excavation, at 20c. per yard	$13.00
882 ft. foundation, at 15c. per ft	132.30
725 ft. foundation, at 10c. per ft	72.50
6,000 bricks in chimneys, at $12 per M	72.00
40 ft. stone steps and coping, at 30c. per ft	12.00
900 yards lath and plastering, at 28c. per yard	252.00
4,799 ft. of timber, at $15 per M	72.00

Sills, 4×8 in. 218 ft. long.	45 beams, 3×8 in. 16 ft. long.
1 girt, 4×8 in. 20 ft. long.	22 beams, 3×8 in. 22 ft. long.
7 posts, 4×7 in. 22 ft. long.	15 beams, 3×7 in. 9 ft. long.
2 posts, 4×7 in. 18 ft. long.	4 valleys, 3×8 in. 20 ft. long.

Ties and plates, 4×6 in. 384 ft. long.

```
500 wall-strips, 2×4 in. 13 ft. long, at 11c. each........  ..............  $55.00
340 novelty siding boards, 9¼ in., at 28c. each..............  ........   95.20
150 lbs. tarred felting, at 5c. per lb..............................  .   7.50
300 matched flooring boards, 9¼ in. wide, at 28c. each................   84.00
 20 rough spruce plank, at 25c. each....  .............................    5.00
270 shingling-lath, at 6c. each...................................  ..   16.20
 48 bunches shingles, at $1.50 each....................................   72.00
 75 hemlock boards, 10-inch, at 18c. each.......  .....................   13.50
 .7 squares of tin roofing, at $9 per square...........  .... .......   63.00
    Materials in cornices and outside casings........................   60.00
 33 narrow pine flooring for front piazza, at 25c. each...............  .    8.25
 67 narrow pine ceiling, at 25c. each.................................   16.75
  1 bay-window, complete.........................................  ....   75.00
 26 plain windows, complete, at $12 each...........................   312.00
  4 cellar windows, complete, at $6 each.............................   24.00
 30 doors, complete, at $10 each.....................................  300.00
    Stairs, complete, $70; 8 closets, fitted complete, $40. .  .........  ..  111.00
  2 marble and 2 pine mantles...........  ...........  ..............   50.00
    Nails, $20 ; range, with elevated oven. $80.....................  100.00
    Plumbing, $84 ; cartage, average 1 mile, $27.08..................  111.08
    Carpenter's labor, not included above............................  250.00
    Painting.......  .........  ...............................  .........  120.00
    Incidentals.......................  ................................   25.72
                                                                        _____
    Total cost, complete...................................................$2,600.00
```

DESIGN XXII.

A HOUSE COSTING $2,800.

This plan of a suburban, or a country house, has all
the advantages of the square form—providing convenient,
commodious interior apartments, and has a simple, expressive outside dress, that compares favorably with more
pretentious, expensive dwellings.... EXTERIOR, (89.)—
The outlines of the main building are rounded and compact, indicating completeness and solidity. The front
tower-like projection is a central and distinctive feature,
around which the other parts are symmetrically balanced.
The Porch and roofed balconies are simple and neat. The
main roof, a new modification of the "Mansard roof," is
a conspicuous part, giving an expression of strength and
unity to the design. The main cornice has full projections, with neat solid trusses, and is separated into sections by the chamber windows, giving relief from the
monotony and depressing effects usual in all continuous
horizontal lines. All the second story windows of the

main building have projecting hoods appropriately interlaced with the principal roof work, securing pleasant
shadows to those parts, and imparting a marked finish

Fig. 89.—FRONT ELEVATION.

and variety. The dormer windows are triangular, and
are placed immediately above those of the lower stories,
prolonging the vertical lines of openings, to which they
form a fitting termination.... FIRST STORY, (fig. 90.)—
Hight of ceiling, 10 feet. The usual front hall is dis-
pensed with, and the stairway is placed where it is more
convenient and accessible, and is not a conductor of cold
drafts through the house. Many think it necessary to
have stairways share with the parlors the most valuable
and conspicuous position ; they should more frequently

be placed in some subordinate relation, without seeming
to control the general arrangement. The entrance from
the front porch is through double doors to the vestibule,
and thence to either the parlor or family-room. Side
doors lead to the pleasant and shady front balconies.
The Parlor and Family-room are of equal size, and may

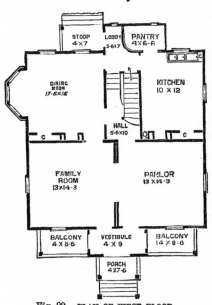

be used as one spa-
cious apartment by
opening the sliding
doors. The Din-
ing-room is pleas-
antly situated, and
opens into the fam-
ily-room, rear en-
trance, and hall-
way. It has one
large bay-window,
and two plain ones,
an open fire-place,
and a dish or china
closet, c. The
Kitchen is isolated,
relieving other
rooms of its noise
and odors, is con-
venient to the din-
ing-room, cellar-

Fig. 90.—PLAN OF FIRST FLOOR.

stairway, and rear entrance, through the rear lobby, and
has an open fire-place, closet, and large pantry, range,
boiler, sink, wash-tubs, and the necessary pipes for water.
The hall is central, accessible from the parlor, dining-
room, and rear entrance, and is thoroughly lighted and
ventilated by the window at the head of the stairs.....
SECOND STORY, fig. 91.)—Hight of ceiling, 8 feet. This
story contains a hall, four good-sized chambers, with closets, and two windows to each. The Bath-room has bath-

tub and seat. A
Conservatory
connects through
sash doors with
the two front
chambers.......
ATTIC, (fig. 92.)
—Hight of ceil-
ing, 8 feet. The
stairs to this are
placed immedi-
ately above those
to the second
story, are ceiled
in, with a door at
the bottom. The
rear portion is

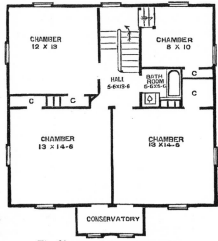

Fig. 91.—PLAN OF SECOND FLOOR.

finished on a line with the two chimneys, into two bedrooms and a hall. The front portion is floored, but oth-

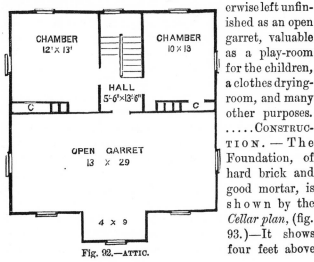

Fig. 92.—ATTIC.

erwise left unfin-
ished as an open
garret, valuable
as a play-room
for the children,
a clothes drying-
room, and many
other purposes.
.....CONSTRUC-
TION. — The
Foundation, of
hard brick and
good mortar, is
shown by the
Cellar plan, (fig.
93.)—It shows
four feet above

the grade in front, and, if desirable, may show one-half that hight in the rear. There is usually sufficient earth taken from the cellar excavations to give such desirable grade as shall turn off all water from the immediate grounds and walks. The chimneys are also of hard brick, are independent of the foundations, and are carried

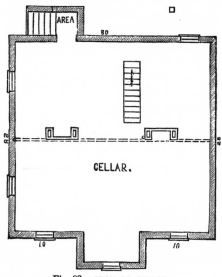

Fig. 93.—PLAN OF CELLAR.

up perfectly plumb to the roof, where they are finished with neat bases and caps. The central position of these chimneys is proof against cold-air openings at their sides, and insures saving the heat radiated from them. It is impossible to prevent cracks from appearing along the sides of chimneys in frame buildings, and when these cracks communicate directly with the outside covering, they often admit much cold air.—The principal frame is 20 ft. high, substantially constructed, as indicated by the upright section (fig. 94). The main plates are in line

with the beams of the attic story, and the roof-purlins
are 8 feet above them. The side-rafters are 12 feet long,
fitted and spiked to the purlins and
plates, with their lower ends extending 2½ feet down from the latter in a
continuous line. Rough brackets connecting the rafters with the upright
frame-work, forming the foundations
or frame of the principal cornice. By
this method of extending the rafters
downward instead of upward, the desirable hight and proportion of roof
are obtained. The exposed surfaces
that require siding are reduced from
the usual hight of 22½ feet to 16 feet,
and the cornices are more substantial
and less complex. The siding, roof-
boarding, slating, and trimming are
done in the usual manner. The gutters are laid in with the slate, as described in Design V. The hoods and
dormer windows have slate coverings,

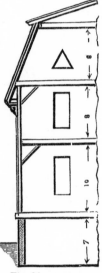

Fig. 94.—SECTION.

interlaced with the principal roof, with joinings and flash-
ings of sheet-lead. The following estimate provides for
the thorough completion of the building in an appropriate and substantial manner.—ESTIMATE :

82 yards excavation, at 20c. per yard	$16.40
16,000 brick. furnished and laid, at $12 per M	192.00
44 ft. stone steps, coping, etc.. at 30c. per ft	13.20
750 yards plastering. at 28c. per yard	210.00
3,497 ft. timber. at $15 per M	52.45

1 sill. 4×8 in. 116 ft. long.	1 perline, 3×7 in. 96 ft. long.
1 girt. 4×8 in. 30 ft. long.	48 beams, 2×8 in. 14 ft. long.
11 posts. 4×7 in. 19 ft. long.	24 beams, 2×8 in. 18 ft. long.
1 tie. 4×6 in. 116 ft. long.	27 beams, 2×8 in. 15 ft. long.
1 plate. 4×6 in. 138 ft. long.	1 stoop, 3×7 in. 70 ft. long.

30 rafters. 3×4 in. 13 ft.. at 16c. each	4.80
380 wall-strips. at 11c. each	41.80
200 siding. 10-inch. at 26c. each	52.00
Materials in cornices and corner-boards	50.00
261 hemlock roof-boards. at 16c. each	41.76
19 squares of slating. at $9 per square	171.00
8 squares of tinning (I. C. charcoal). at $7 per square	56.00
250 ft. gutters and leaders. at 8c. per ft	20.00
300 flooring. 9×1¼ in., at 26c. each	78.00

200 lbs. felting, at 3c. per lb	$6.00
3 stairs, complete	75.00
Porch, balconies, and stoops, complete	160.00
6 cellar windows, $36; 1 bay window, complete, $60	96.00
12 plain windows, $144; 9 hooded windows, complete, $135	279.00
8 dormer windows, complete, at $8 each	64.00
32 doors, at $9.50 each, $304; 7 closets, complete, $14	318.00
3 marble mantles, $60; 3 marble shelves, complete, $18	78.00
Range and plumbing, complete	188.09
Well, from bath-room to roof, complete	15.00
Gas-pipes for 18 lights, complete	40.00
Bells and speaking-tubes, complete	20.00
Finish of part of attic, complete	60.00
Nails, $24; cartage, average 1 mile, $25	49.00
Carpenter's labor, not included above	150.00
Painting, 2 coats, complete	150.00
Incidentals	52.50
Total cost, complete	$2,800.00

DESIGN XXIII.

A COUNTRY OR VILLAGE HOUSE, COSTING $2,800.— FOR PHYSICIANS, LAWYERS, CLERGYMEN, JUS-TICES, NOTARIES, EDITORS, ETC.

This plan is designed to meet the wants of a large class residing in the country, or smaller villages, who are not only directly interested in agricultural pursuits, but who have also some professional or official vocation, such as : Physicians, Lawyers, Justices, Notaries, Clergymen, etc. They require in connection with their residences an apart-ment adapted to their special callings, that shall in no way interfere with their domestic arrangements, where all persons making business calls may enter without feel-ing that they are intruding on the privacy of the house-hold..... ELEVATION, (fig. 95.)—The exterior outlines and dress of this plan are a fair representation of the pre-vailing styles of American rural house architecture, in its most genteel and practical forms. There is a manifest propriety in the strong and decided features of the exte-rior finish of this example, wherein each part has its dis-tinctive characteristics of utility, harmony, and truthfulness—a combination that never fails to please even the most tasteful, and it may therefore be regarded as the real basis of beauty. We frequently meet with oddly-proportioned country houses, evidently constructed with a sole regard to utility, that present a stunted and cadav-

Fig. 95.—ELEVATION OF HOUSE, WITH OFFICE ATTACHED.

erous appearance, having been shorn of their beauty through a mistaken idea that *economy* precludes the least indulgence in taste. Good taste only demands that every separate part of any building shall be in harmony with the whole, and this feature of harmony is not so much a subject of expense as of expression, being a result of *mode* rather than the *matter* of construction. The materials necessarily required for any building assume shape and expression according to the methods of their application, and they may be applied in disproportion, so as to be of permanent disgrace ; whereas the same materials properly and intelligently used, with a like expense of handling, develop into proportionate and expressive forms of elegance and grace. A building constructed as indicated by these plans presents a pleasing appearance from any direction, each face being broken by wings or other pro-

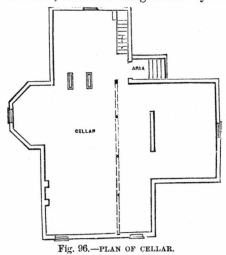

jections, which give relief from the formalities of a large, flat surface. From the front there is an expression of completeness indicating full provision for comfort, and an air* of contentment. From the sides are presented to the best advantage the more ex-

Fig. 96.—PLAN OF CELLAR.

tended surfaces, including the large corniced gables of the principal building, the rear wing, and other projections. The rear has an equally finished and satisfactory appearance..... THE CELLAR (fig. 96), is the full size of the ground-plans, with a clear hight of 7 feet. The five cellar windows are placed where they will admit light to every part. An outside entrance is under the rear lobby, and a stairway leads directly to the kitchen...... FIRST STORY, (fig. 97.)—The arrangement is very simple and convenient, comprising good-sized hall, parlor, living-room, kitchen, office, study, five closets, and two stair-

ways, with ceilings 10 feet high. The Parlor is pleasantly situated, has two front windows opening directly to
the piazza, from which they derive shade and protection.
The Dining or living-room opens into the hall, parlor,
and kitchen, and has two closets. One end of this room
is octagonal, and extends 6 feet beyond the face of the
principal, with three windows, affording a pleasant outlook. The Kitch-
en adjoins the
dining-room, has
two closets, is fit-
ted up with a
range, sink, and
wash-tubs, and is
conveniently
connected with
the cellar and
with second story
by private stair-
ways. The Office
is entered from
the front porch,
and is in direct
communication
with the princi-
pal hall, has a
good-sized closet
from the space

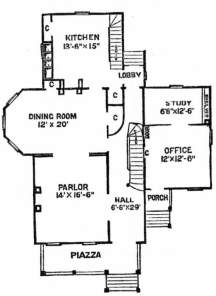

Fig. 97.—PLAN OF FIRST FLOOR.

under the principal stairs, and has a private room or
Study.... SECOND STORY, (fig. 98.)—This is divided into
four commodious apartments, beside a hall, bath-room,
and the necessary closets, and has ceilings 8 feet high in
the main building, and 7 feet in the rear wing. The
Bath-room is provided with a seat-closet and bath-tub.
An inclosed stairway leads to the Attic, where two or
more bedrooms may be finished, besides leaving space for

garret purposes. The tank placed over the ceiling of the bath-room is arranged to receive water from the principal roof, and is provided with an overflow pipe leading to the cistern..... GENERAL REQUIREMENTS.—Full brick foundations are estimated for. Where coarse stone can be had, they answer as well, and at less cost, for the portions below ground ; they should be laid even with the brick-work on the inside when finished. The wood-work

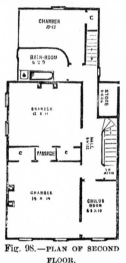

is to be substantially constructed of good and sufficient materials throughout. The roofs of the piazza, stoop, bay, lobby, and window caps, are covered with charcoal tin, and in each case an allowance is made for a "flashing" of 6 inches in width to turn up behind the siding, to prevent leakage. The principal and the two wing roofs are each covered with dark slate with ridge plates of zinc. The gutters are to be those described for Design V. The joinings of the wing-roofs against the main building are made perfectly

Fig. 98.—PLAN OF SECOND FLOOR.

tight by laying in, against the building, right angle strips of zinc or tin "flashing," with each course of slate before the siding is put on. Slate is unquestionably the best material for such roofing when the form of roof will admit of its use ; its cost is the same as for good tinning, and about 2 cents per square foot in excess of pine shingles ; when once properly done, will last for centuries; it is fire-proof, and the water from it is much purer, an important consideration when rain and cistern water is used for cooking or drinking. Its color and appearance are agreeable—in fact roofs of other materials are often painted in imitation of slate from choice..... The most expressive portions of any buildings are their projecting cornices. As a rule, for houses of this style, such projections should be *one inch for every foot of their hight from the foundation.* And the same rule will apply to every detail of the exterior finish; for example, as in this case, the principal building being 22 feet high at the plate, the principal cornices should project 22 inches; the piazza being 11 feet high, its cornice projects 11 inches; the windows, 6 feet high, have caps projecting 6 inches, etc. By this simple rule, all such projections may be readily determined, and thus secure perfect proportion and harmony of parts.... The inside plastering is *" three-coat work."* All side-walls should be continued down *close* to the floor, to prevent the passage of air or sound. Care should be taken to make the walls straight and true, with the second coat of *" browning,"* for the last or white coat, though applied in the best manner, can never overcome malformations in the body of the plastering; on the contrary, the finer the finish of last coat, the more visibly will such defects appear. In the concluding estimate, 28 cents per yard is allowed for the cost of plastering, which is ample, as shown by these calculations *for* 100 *yards,* viz. :

2,000 lath, at $2 per M	$4.00
10 lbs. lath-nails, at 6c. per lb	60
4 barrels lime, at $1 per barrel	4.00
5 loads sand, at 30c. per load	1.50
1 barrel finishing lime, at $1.40 per barrel	1.40
1¼ bushel plaster, 37c.; 1 bushel hair, 50c	87
Cartage	3.00
Labor putting on lath, at 10c. per bunch	2 00
¾ day laborer (mixing mortar), at $1.50 per day	75
1½ days mason (work), at $2.50 per day	3.75
1¼ days laborer (" tending " mason), at $1.50 per day	2.25
Use of screen, water barrel, and scaffolding	1.00
Total cost for 100 square yards, complete	$25.12
Incidentals	2.88
Estimated at 28c. per yard	$28.00

In some localities, a practice prevails among masons of including in their measurements of plastering one-half of the openings of doors and windows, which is obviously

unjust, and a frequent cause of dispute. Such openings
will average at least 2 yards each—in this house would
aggregate 50 yards—and in every case should be deduct-
ed, unless otherwise agreed previously.—ESTIMATE :

113 yards, excavation, at 20c. per yard	$22.60
12,000 brick, laid complete, at $12 per M	144.00
47 ft. stone steps and coping, at 30c. per ft	14.10
841 yards plastering, at 28c. per yard	235.48
5,135 ft. timber, at $15 per M	77.02

1 sill, 4×8 in. 200 ft. long.	Plates, 4×6 in. 100 ft. long.
1 girder, 4×8 in. 30 ft. long.	Ties, 4×6 in. 330 ft. long.
7 posts, 4×7 in. 21 ft. long.	1 ridge, 3×7 in. 26 ft. long.
2 posts, 4×7 in. 18 ft. long.	20 rafters, 3×5 in. 20 ft. long.
2 posts, 4×6 in. 12 ft. long.	35 beams, 3×8 in. 22 ft. long.
Piazza, 3×8 in. 82 ft. long.	9 beams, 3×8 in. 19 ft. long.
Piazza, 3×5 in. 40 ft. long.	21 beams, 3×8 in. 13 ft. long.

4 locust posts in cellar, at 30c. each	1.20
375 wall-strips, 2×4 in. at 11c. each	41.25
170 lbs. tarred paper or felting, at 3c. per lb.	5.10
330 siding, 10-inch, at 28c. each	92.40
Materials in cornices, water-table, etc	50.00
213 hemlock boards (for roofing), at 20c. each	42.60
18½ squares slate roofing, at $9 per square	166.50
3 squares tin, at $8 per square	24.00
300 flooring, 9 in., at 28c. each	84.00
Stairs, complete	100.00
5 cellar windows, complete, at $6 each	30.00
18 plain windows, complete, at $12 each	216.00
35 doors, complete, at $10 each	350.00
Piazza, porch, and lobby, complete	150.00
4 mantles, complete, at $20 each	80.00
Closet finish, complete	25.00
Range and elevated oven, etc., complete	80.00
Plumbing, complete	175.00
Bells and speaking-tubes, complete	15.00
Nails, $25; painting, $200; carting, $35	260.00
Carpenter's labor, not included above	223.83
Incidentals	94.92
Total cost, complete	$2,800.00

DESIGN XXIV.

A FARM-HOUSE COSTING $2,800.

This plan will be recognized as comprehending the
general characteristics of those given in Designs XXI.
and XXVI. It is designed to be constructed of similar
materials, with a like variety of pleasing and decided outlines, and to give an equal amount of accommodation and
convenience. The division and arrangement of the sev-

eral parts, however, are entirely changed, being especially
intended to meet the requirements of a location having a
western frontage. Location is an important consideration, involving many questions of adaptation, that should
always guide to the selection of such a plan as will express a natural fitness for the situation, and truthfully
indicate its purpose..... EXTERIOR, (fig. 99.)—Only two

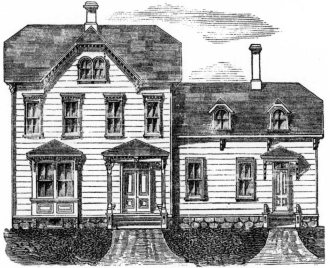

Fig. 99.—ELEVATION OF FARM-HOUSE.

feet of the foundation-walls are exposed to sight, which
brings the frame-work of the building quite near enough
to the ground. The surface of the earth surrounding
such buildings should have a grade of *at least* one-half
inch to the foot, for the distance of 50 feet in every direction, to insure the turning away of all surface water
from the walks and grounds. Another good result de-
rived from such grade is the additional altitude given to
the building, imparting a much better appearance. The
general outlines of the elevation are very simple, devoid

of all pretentious ornamentation. The wide frontage,
the large and numerous openings, and ample roofs, are
each expressive of frankness and hospitality, eminently
befitting the home of the farmer. The front Porch is
unusually wide, and arranged to have large columns, and
stationary seats at either side. The Bay-window has
square projections, instead of octagonal, which are equally
appropriate in this case, and less costly. The cornices of
the principal building project 20 inches, and those of the
wing 16 inches, and both are provided with scroll-sawed
trusses. The chimney-tops are large, and heavily capped.
The same general finish, as is shown on the front, is put

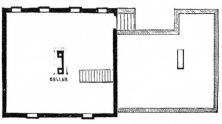

on the sides and
rear, so that the
building pre-
sents an equally
complete and
satisfactory ap-
pearance from
every direction.
Buildings of this
character should

Fig. 100.—PLAN OF CELLAR.

be set back from the street line at least 50 feet—150 feet
would be much better—to give room for trees, shrubbery,
and walks..... CELLAR, (fig. 100.)—The plans provide
for a cellar under the principal building only, which gives
a clear space of 22×25 feet. If desired, the space beneath
the wing may be included at an additional cost of $65.
The excavations for the cellar in the earth is 3 feet 8
inches deep ; this allows the foundation-walls to be 7 feet
high. The earth thrown out is to be graded around the
building to the hight of $1\frac{1}{2}$ foot, thus leaving two feet
of the foundation exposed on the outside. Country
houses are frequently set so low down as to be a matter of
regret ever afterwards. There are constant accumula-
tions of dust, and other matter, caught and held by the

shrubbery and grasses, so that there is soon discovered a
seeming growth of the earth upward around the house
and immediate grounds, making it impossible to adapt
the grades that are desirable. It is far better that foundations are a little too high than too low, for when too
high, the approaches can easily be raised at any time with
a few loads of earth ; but when too low, there seems to
be no cure, except to raise the entire building.   The
foundation-walls are designed to be constructed of broken
stone, laid in coarse mortar, as more particularly described
for Design XXI..... FIRST STORY, (fig. 101.)—Hight of
ceilings, 10 ft.
Entire floor
measurement,
1,206 s q u a r e
feet, affording
ample space for
g o o d - s i z e d
apartments.
The several di-
visions have es-
pecial regard to

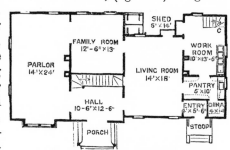

Fig. 101.—PLAN OF FIRST FLOOR.

comfort and convenience.   The front hall, or reception
room, is nearly square, of good dimensions, is entered
from the front porch through double or folding doors,
and adjoins the parlor and living-room, and contains the
principal stairs.   The Parlor is unusually large, is provided with windows in its sides, and has stucco cornices
and centers in its ceilings, with an arched finish in the
bay-window.   The Living, or Dining-room, is commodious, pleasantly situated, with outlooks front and rear,
and is easily accessible all around.   The Family-room is
large, connects with the dining-room and parlor, and is
intended as a sitting or sewing-room.   If occasion require, this room might be used as the bed-room of an
invalid.   The Work-room, or Kitchen, is conveniently

arranged to have a range, boiler, pump, sink, wash-tubs, and pipes for cold and hot water, and adjoins the dining-room, a large pantry, and a rear entrance door, and has a private stairway leading to the second story, with a closet underneath. The Pantry is of ample dimensions, is conveniently arranged with shelving, and has a zinc wash-tray, with cold and hot water-pipes, and adjoins the kitchen, dining-room, and a china closet. The latter is useful for storing wares not required daily. The rear shed is paved, and the cellar doors are constructed as described for Design XXI.... SECOND STORY, (fig. 102.)—

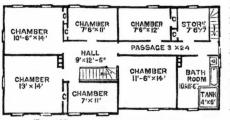

Fig. 102.—PLAN OF SECOND FLOOR.

Hight of ceiling, 9 feet in main building, and 8 feet in wing. Floor measurement, 1,276 feet, divided into 8 good-sized rooms, besides halls, closets, and stairways. The principal hall connects with each chamber in main building, and one room and passage in wing. The door between the principal hall and wing-passage may be closed at any time, cutting off communication at pleasure. The side, or "breast" walls, in the wing, are vertical 3 feet, and are continued upward at an angle of 45° to the ceiling, thus securing sufficient head-room. The bath-room is exactly above the kitchen, and contains a tank, bath-tub, and seat-closet, with pipes for cold and hot water..... ATTIC.—The stairs to this are over the first flight, and are designed to be neatly ceiled in with $4\frac{1}{2}$-inch beaded ceiling-boards, with a door at the foot. Double windows in each gable admit sufficient light, and afford ventilation..... REMARKS ON CONSTRUCTION.—An insight into the character of this plan, is best had by carefully consid-

ering the materials and cost in the estimate added. We
would urge the importance of good methods and work-
manship in construction, without which all materials,
however good or sufficient, can never produce good results. The old maxim, " whatever is worth doing at all,
is worth doing well," especially applies to building a home
in which one is to spend a lifetime. This does not imply
extravagance in any sense, only demanding such *careful
and intelligent application of the ordinary rules of construction*, as shall insure substantial work, that will not
be a continuous source of anxiety and expense. Any one
of ordinary intelligence should be able to generally superintend the operations of the mechanics employed in constructing a farm-house. The following *points* are of the
greatest importance. Carefully watch that the foundation-walls are substantially laid, and accurately leveled on
their upper surfaces, so that the doors shall not strike the
floor or carpets in opening, nor the tables, chairs, or
other furniture be obliged to stand on three legs. The
frame-work, when raised, should be plumb, so that all
work on or in the building can be cut square, and applied
without tedious fitting. The siding should be thoroughly "seasoned" in the open air before using, and
carefully applied with close joints, and well nailed. The
edges of all water-tables, corner-boards, and window-
frames should be painted *before* setting. The shingles
should be carefully laid, breaking their joints at one-third
of their width, and double nailed. The flooring should
be dry, close laid, and nailed with two nails to each beam.
The partitions should be set with studding of selected
widths ; and their angles or corners should be anchored
firmly together, to prevent the walls from cracking in
those parts when finished. The chimneys should be carefully constructed ; all joints between the brick-work
should be surely filled with mortar, to prevent sparks
from passing through to the frame-work. All mortar for

7

plastering should be properly mixed, and allowed sufficient time (at least one week), for the thorough slaking
of the lime, and a complete permeation of its caustic
properties. Thin coats of plastering are better than
heavy ones. A mortar that does not crack in setting or
drying is sure to be good. The interior wood finish
should not be commenced until the plastering is completely dried out, and all loose mortar is removed from
the building. All wood-work usually painted should be
primed as soon as in position. For more explicit remarks
and sundry suggestions on painting, see Design XIII.

Estimate of Materials and Cost :

110 yards excavation, at 20c. per yard	$22.00
1,371 ft. stone foundation, at 15c. per ft	205.65
3,000 brick, furnished and laid, at $12 per M	36.00
46 ft. stone steps, sills, and coping, at 30c. per ft	13.80
1,030 yards plastering, complete, at 28c. per yard	288.40
5,713 ft. timber, at $15 per M	85.69

1 sill, 4×8 in. 186 ft. long.	2 girts, 4×8 in. 25 ft. long.
6 posts, 4×7 in. 21 ft. long.	57 beams, 3×8 in. 25 ft. long.
3 posts, 4×7 in. 14 ft. long.	36 beams, 3×8 in. 13 ft. long.
1 tie, 4×6 in. 256 ft. long.	24 beams, 3×8 in. 11 ft. long.
1 plate, 4×6 in. 186 ft. long.	3 valleys, 3×8 in. 20 ft. long.

24 rafters, 3×5 in. 16 ft. long.

100 joist, 3×4 in. 13 ft. long, at 16c. each	16.00
300 wall-strips, 2×4 in. 13 ft., at 11c. each	33.00
Materials in water-table and cornices	50.00
300 novelty siding-boards, 9¼ in., at 28c. each	84.00
400 shingling-lath, at 6c. each	24.00
69 bunches shingles, at $1.50 per bunch	103.50
84 ft. gutters, 132 ft. leaders, and 134 ft. porch roofs, 10c. per ft	35.00
355 flooring, 9¼×13, at 28c. each	99.40
Porch and hood, complete	75.00
Stairs, complete	90.00
Bay-window, complete	60.00
20 windows, complete, at $10 each	200.00
6 cellar windows, complete, at $6 each	36.00
4 dormer windows, complete, at $20 each	80.00
32 doors, complete, at $10 each	320.00
1 cellar door and hatchway doors	20.00
Shelving and hooks in closets	20.00
2 marble mantles and 4 shelves with trusses	75.00
Range and plumbing, complete	215.00
Nails	25.00
Bells and speaking-tubes	20.00
Painting	150.00
Cartage, 1 mile	35.00
Carpenter's labor, not included above	250.00
Incidentals	32.56
Total cost, complete	$2,800.00

D E S I G N   X X V .

Fig. 103.—FRONT VIEW OF HOUSE.

A "HALF STONE" HOUSE FOR $2,800

This plan is designed for a substantial, convenient, and inexpensive country house. It has two full finished stories, with well-lighted apartments of good size, and a large cellar and attic. It has also the merit of architectural beauty, well adapted to a commanding location....
EXTERIOR, (fig. 103.)—The "half-stone" composition of the side walls, and the strong outlines and slating of the main roof, give to this structure a rustic, yet substantial appearance, affording both diversity and picturesqueness, as shown in the variety of the openings and irregularity of the several parts. The front and rear elevations are similar; by changing the entrance doors and stairs, either

side may front the road. The details of exterior finish
are so simple, and easy of execution, that any "modification for the rear" is undesirable. Inharmonious and unsightly curtailments in the rear finish have a depressing
influence on those obliged to face them daily, which can
never be overcome by knowing there is a good front......
CELLAR, (fig. 104.)—Hight, $6\frac{1}{2}$ feet, of which $4\frac{1}{2}$ feet
is below the ground surface, and therefore (with its
thick walls),
frost proof.
It is always
important to
provide for
carrying off
the poisonous
vapors apt to
be generated
in cellars.
For this pur-
pose side
openings are
made near
the ceiling in-

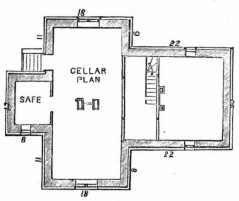

Fig 104.—PLAN OF CELLAR.

to one of the flues of each chimney. These flues, extending to the top, and warmed by contact with the fires of
the upper stories, have sufficient draft to constantly
change the cellar air, and prevent its ascent through the
living-rooms.... FIRST STORY, (fig. 105.)—Hight of ceilings, 10 feet. Here are conveniently placed three large
rooms, a hall, china closet, and large pantry. Each large
room has commodious windows with views in two directions. The pleasant piazzas at both the front and rear of
the parlor, extend over and protect the entrance doors.
.... SECOND STORY, (fig. 106.)—Hight of ceilings, 8 feet.
The divisions are very simple, a hall, four chambers, four
closets, and a bath-room. Light railings may be put on

the roofs of the wings and piazzas to form pleasant balconies to the windows of this story. One such balcony is
shown over the wing-roof (fig. 103) ; the others may be
similar. The small cost of these devices is fully repaid
in their usefulness for airing purposes, besides imparting
a cheerful appearance.... GARRET OR ATTIC.—This story
is thoroughly floored, but otherwise unfinished. Should
additional chambers be required, partitions may be set
over those or the second story, duplicating that plan,
with rooms having the same hight of ceilings. The stairs

are placed im-
mediately
above those of
the lower sto-
ries, are ceiled
in, and have a
door at the
foot.... CON-
STRUCTION. —
The durabil-
ity, general
abundance,
and substan-

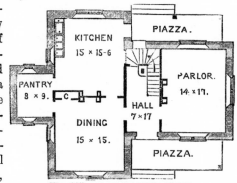

Fig. 105.—PLAN OF FIRST FLOOR.

tial appearance of stone, make it the most desirable and
appropriate material known for the exterior walls of any
building. The cost of cutting and dressing such material ready for use is the principle barrier to its general
adoption. By using bricks for corners and for the finish
around the openings, the most expensive item of stone-
work is saved. They need only to be " random dressed,"
and laid nearly in the shape in which they are quarried,
as more particularly described for Design XXVII. When
such walls are carried beyond the hight that is convenient for the handling of the materials, the expense of
their construction is largely increased. It is for this
reason that the " half-stone " method is particularly val-

uable. In this plan, the stone-work extends only to the
hight of the ceiling of the first story ; to this hight the
materials may be readily wheeled on trestled scaffolding,
while to double this hight would require the use of the
tedious derrick, and additional help. The upper stories
are framed of the usual sized timber, and raised on the
stone walls, which in this case become their foundation.
The main roof is constructed as shown in Design XXII.
The hight requiring siding is $4^1/_2$ feet, or including water-
table and cornice, $6^1/_2$ feet from the stone-work of the

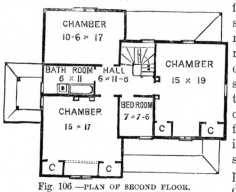

first story to the
slating of the
r o o f .   T h e
main roof cov-
ering is of dark
s l a t e laid on
tarred felt. At
or near the
floor-line divid-
ing the upper
stories, it is ap-
propriate to in-
dicate the di-

Fig. 106.—PLAN OF SECOND FLOOR.

vision by the use of tinted slate, which may be laid in
close courses or in simple figures, as shown on the eleva-
vation. The roofs of the hooded and dormer windows
are also slated. The deck of the main roof, and the
roofs of the piazza, are covered with I. C. charcoal tin.
The wood-finish is made of simple design, devoid of all
efforts at pretentious display, each part being chosen with
especial regard for its utility and appropriateness. The
trusses, piazza-columns, and soffits are worked of timber
neatly stop-chamfered, imparting a rustic appearance to
them, in keeping with the stone-work. The water-tank
is placed in the attic, directly above and in line with the
bath-tub and kitchen-range, favoring the most practical